Lecture Notes in Economics and Mathematical Systems

Joan Esteban

The Social Viability of Money

Competitive Equilibria and the Core of Overlapping Generations Economies

Springer-Verlag
Berlin Heidelberg New York
London Paris Tokyo
Hong Kong Barcelona
Budapest

Author

Dr. Joan Esteban
Institut d'Anàlisi Econòmica, CSIC
Universitat Autònoma de Barcelona
Bellaterra, E-08193 Barcelona

ISBN 3-540-54649-9 Springer-Verlag Berlin Heidelberg New York
ISBN 0-387-54649-9 Springer-Verlag New York Berlin Heidelberg

Printed in Germany

Typesetting: Camera ready by author
Printing and binding: Druckhaus Beltz, Hemsbach/Bergstr.
42/3140-543210 - Printed on acid-free paper

CONTENTS

Foreword

The content of this book has developed along a fairly extended period of time. It was Teo Millán who by October 1981 drew my attention to overlapping generations models, when conducting a workshop on this topic at the Universitat Autònoma de Barcelona. This workshop was attended by Xavier Calsamiglia, Isabel Fradera, Andreu Mas-Colell, Clara Ponsati and Pep Oliu. It was there were I first presented my initial ideas on the core of an overlapping generations economy with one agent per generation, which finally became what now is the subject of Chapters V and VI, in Part III.

An initial version of the material contained in these Chapters was published at the Working Papers series of the Department and was later converted into two articles: "El núcleo en Economias de Generaciones Sucesivas", Revista Española de Economia, 2 (1985), 3-17, and "A Characterization of the Core in Overlapping-Generations Economies", Journal of Economic Theory 39 (1986), 439-456. The extension of the model to generations with many agents was initiated as a joint work with Teo Millán during the first half of 1983 and has now become Chapter VII of this book. It has been previously published as "Competitive Equilibria and the Core of Overlapping Generations Economies" Journal of Economic Theory 50 (1990), 155-174, co-authored with Teo Millán.

The development of my research has shaped the structure of the book. Except for an introductory Chapter, it is organized in self-contained units. Each Chapter begins with an introductory section, containing the motivation and review of the relevant related work. This is followed by the formal description of the model, as well as the definitions and assumptions that will be used in the Chapter. Finally, chapters end with a section discussing the main implications of the results. In order to help the reader not familiar with the Overlapping Generation model I have included Chapters II, III ad IV, Part II of the book, which give a rigorous but not highly technical presentation of the model.

I wish to aknowledge my debt to the colleagues and friends who have read different bits of my research in previous versions. I have benefited from helpful comments by Jordi Andreu, Salvador Barberá, Dave Cass, Suchan Chae, Luis Corchón, Isabel Fradera, Jean Fraïsse, John Geanakoplos, Birgit Grodal, Roger Guesnerie, Tim Kehoe, Jean-Jacques Laffont, Antonio Manresa, Andreu Mas-Colell, Michel Moreau, Heraklis Polemarchakis, Ferran Sancho, José Scheinkman, Karl Shell, Hugo Sonnenschein, Juan Urrutia, Fernando Vega, and Neil Wallace. I wish to give special thanks to Teo Millán, Xavier Çalsamiglia, David Bevan, Jim Mirrlees and Nick Stern. They have discussed with me virtually every point and have been for me a constant source of stimulus.

Financial support from the *Fundación del Banco Exterior* for the completion of this research is gratefully acknowledged.

PART I

INTRODUCTION

Chapter I The Viability of Fiat Money

I.1. Introduction

In this book we analyse overlapping generations economies from a game theoretical point of view. We are concerned with the social acceptability of consumption allocations in infinite horizon models of pure exchange economies with agents with finite lifetimes who behave cooperatively. Specifically, we study the core of such economies and its relation with competitive equilibria.

The overlapping generations model poses a number of specific theoretical problems. The fundamental difference with respect to the standard Arrow-Debreu model is the description of the population of consumers. In the overlapping generations model time is defined as an indefinite sequence of periods. In each period a new generation is born and a generation dies. Let us suppose that periods are so defined that every generation lives for two periods. Generation t when young will overlap with old generation t-1 and when old with the then new young generation t+1. This specific demographic structure imposes an exogenously given interdependence among consumers. Exchanges involving future deliveries against present goods can only be agreed under the certainty that the future unborn generation will accept to carry out the delivery which in turn requires the certainty that the generation after will in turn make a compensating delivery, and so on.

Samuelson [50] was the first to give an example of an overlapping generations model in which the walrasian equilibrium was not Pareto optimal. Since then there have been many contributions towards explaining why the competitive mechanism may fail in bringing about efficient allocations. Amongst the most significant ones we have Cass and Yaari [14], Shell [55], Gale [27], Balasko and Shell [4] and Okuno and Zilcha [47]. The fact that the First Fundamental Theorem of Welfare Economics does not apply to overlapping generations economies makes plain that some walrasian allocations will be unanimously rejected by the full sequence of consumers. Therefore, it is obvious that there is another way in which the overlapping generations model departs from standard Arrow-Debreu economies. The well known result that the set of competitive equilibria is a subset of the set of core allocations (and as the economy is replicated it coincides with) will not apply either. It is our purpose to provide a detailed examination of this point.

Since Samuelson's [50] contribution overlapping generations models have been seen as the appropriate framework in which the "social contrivance of money" could be examined. The introduction of fiat money permits the implementation of Pareto optimum allocations that could not have been reached in barter economies. The question arises of whether the institution of fiat money is a stable one, i.e. will not be refused by some agents. In Samuelson's [50] words «the use of money can itself be regarded as a social compact» (p.482). But, as he points out, «in terms of immediate self-interest the existing productive workers should perhaps unilaterally repudiate the money upon which the aged hope to live in retirement. So a continuing social compact is required» (ibid. ,p.482, footnote 22). Besides their relevance for the foundations of monetary theory, these questions may shed some light on problems of our real economies. Hyper-inflations can be interpreted as a lack of confidence or as a rejection of fiat money as a store of value.[1]

The social acceptability of institutions created by governments in order to intervene in the working of market economies has not been an object of analysis for Public Economics. The standard problem in Public Economics is the optimal (from the point of view of some Social valuation function) correction of the inefficiencies created by specific market imperfections. In that case it is obvious that any second best allocation would be unanimously rejected by cooperative agents. Therefore, there seems to be little scope for progress by using a cooperative game theoretical approach.

One of the distinct characteristics of overlapping generations economies is that the type of governmental interventions mentioned above can bring about first best allocations and the previous argument does not apply. From this point of view our research can be seen as providing an answer to the following question: given that in overlapping generations economies allocations resulting from governmental intervention are not necessarily rejected by cooperative agents, can we prove that indeed there exist acceptable interventions? are there limits beyond which public interventions become rejected?. However, we do not attempt at giving a complete answer to these complex problems. We only try to make a first step by providing a purely theoretical analysis in a simple overlapping generations model. From an abstract point of view, this kind of question calls for a game theoretical analysis and, as we shall argue, the cooperative behaviour of agents seems a natural way of starting the study of these problems in an infinite horizon, overlapping generations model.[2]

The use of the theory of cooperative games for analysing the social credibility or trustworthiness of consumption allocations is not new. Douglas Gale [28] and [29] has modelled the notion of lack of trust in a two period economy and identified the sequential core as the set of trustworthy allocations. As we shall discuss at length in Chapters VI and VII, in spite of the substantial difference between the two models, our results can be interpreted as providing a rationale for why in his model agents should not trust allocations involving an income transfer from one period to the next.

Much closer to our research are the papers by Hendricks, Judd and Kovenock [36], Kovenock [43] and Chae [16]. These works analyse the core of pure exchange, overlapping generations economies for the case of one consumer, many consumers and a continuum of consumers per generation , respectively. Their contributions will be reported in detail and duly related with our results in the corresponding Chapters.

The main contributions, contained in Part III, Chapters V to VII, are preceeded by the presentation of the Overlapping Generation model and the most significant results concerning efficiency and existence of Walrasian and monetary equilibria. This introduction to the Overlapping Generations model is the object of Part II, Chapters II, III and IV.

The remainder of this introductory Chapter is organized as follows. In the next section we argue about the opportunity of studying cooperative games in overlapping generations models. The main results of our research are summarized in section I.3. The last three sections are devoted to the discussion of the relevance of our results for different areas of Economic Theory. We first explain the possible relevance of our contributions for the theory of general competitive equilibrium. Then, in section I.5. , we go into the implications for the theory of fiat money. Finally, in the last section of this Chapter, we argue that our work can shed some light on the institutional insights of Samuelson when considering money as an implicit social contract.

I.2 Cooperative Games in Overlapping Generations Economies

Whilst in the Arrow-Debreu model agents have no age, a distinctive feature of the overlapping generations model is the explicit treatment of the fact of nature that agents have a finite lifespan and that consequently at any date there will coexist agents at different points of their life cycle. We thus have an infinite string of generations each of which overlaps with its neighbouring generations.

The essential problem we wish to focus on is that in Overlapping Generations economies decisions corresponding to subsequent generations are taken sequentially. For a decision to be taken on sound grounds today we need to foresee whether it would be compatible with the expected decisions of unborn rational agents. A bargaining problem between agents of two coexisting generations needs to take into consideration whether the proposed solution would obtain the implicit agreement of all future generations. It is in this sense that it seems natural to consider that agents behave as if they were cooperating, quite independently of the actual possibility of meeting. This is in sketch the assumption we shall make about individual behaviour as far as the structure of the game is concerned.

Let us assume that there is full information, that is, that every agent knows the preferences and endowments of all future generations. A trade proposal from agent 0 to agent 1 consists of a sequence of consumption allocations c . In order to decide whether to accept it or not agent 1 will have to consider not only the potentially beneficial reallocations of the consumption goods, but the overall viability of the proposed allocation as well. As we have pointed out before, the viability of intertemporal consumption allocations needs the willingness to trade of the subsequent generations of consumers. Therefore, the decision problem can be usefully divided into two steps: i) whether there is a better alternative allocation and ii) whether it is trustworthy, i.e. whether future generations will cooperate. The first step consists in exploring alternative consumption allocations c' which would be as trustworthy as c and which would leave him better off and which might exclude some agents. By ensuring the same degree of trustworthiness we mean that we expect cooperation of the agents to which the reallocation provides at least the same level of utility and that a non-cooperative reaction (i.e. no trade) is expected from the agents which would experience a utility loss. This corresponds to a maximin behaviour in the sense that agents expect the worst possible reponse from ill-treated players.

Let us follow the calculations of agent 1 with some detail. He starts by considering whether there is an improving reallocation of goods of period 1 only. If it is possible for him to be better off while preserving the utility level of agent 0, he will certainly reject the initial consumption allocation because there is an alternative allocation which gives higher utility to himself as is at least as acceptable for the rest of the players as the initial one. Of course, if the initial allocation is weakly Pareto optimal no such reallocation exists and any alternative consumption allocation in which agent 1 is better off will necessarily entail excluding agent 0 from the reallocation. In that case, his consumption allocation in period 1 will be his endowments and thus in order to grant a higher utility level he will have to consider changes in the consumption of period 2 as well. He will have to check then whether that reallocation gives agent 2 at least as much utility as with c while being as trustworthy. This will in turn lead to the examination of the behaviour of agent 3. This mental exercise will go on until agent 1 finds that for the proposed reallocation there exists an agent T who can obtain as much utility as before even if agent T+1 does not cooperate. He can then stop his calculations and safely refuse the initial allocation. Alternatively it might be the case in which he would need to repeat the calculations for the full sequence of agents and find that it would be acceptable to all of them. In that case too agent 1 can confidently reject the initial consumption allocation.

After all these calculations agent 1 might find no preferable consumption allocation which is as trustworthy as the initial allocation. Yet in order to accept the proposed consumption allocation he must still verify whether that allocation is trustworthy, that is, whether any future agent will find it rational not to cooperate. If this was the case for agent t, agent $t-1$ would know and would thus reject the proposal. Therefore that allocation would not be trustworthy for agent 1.

It is easy to realize that all these calculations made by agent 1 amount to verifying whether a given allocation belongs to the core of a cooperative game in which coalitions are restricted to the case of a chain of generations. The proposed consumption allocation will not be acceptable to agent 1 if there exists a subset of future agents that by forming a coalition can improve upon this allocation. The sequential structure of the model imposes that only those allocations that are acceptable for all unborn generations can be acceptable for any two coexisting agents. The main point is that even though the whole sequence of contracts cannot be signed today, any two coexisting rational agents will behave as if these contracts could actually be agreed upon by all agents. This is the reason why we find it justifiable to talk of coalitions.

In an overlapping generations economy coalitions suffer from two specific features. On the one hand, the demographic structure of the economy imposes the natural condition that coalitions are constrained to be formed by agents belonging to subsequent generations, thus being obliged to form a "chain". On this respect our analysis can be related to the papers by Aumann and Drèze [2] and Myerson [46]. These authors examine the core of economies in which blocking coalitions cannot be freely formed, but are subject to some pre-specified structures. From this standpoint, the description of an economy as formed by a sequence of overlapping generations can be seen as a natural justification of their assumption that coalition formation is subject to constraints.

On the other hand, this collection of overlapping generations form an open ended sequence extending indefinitely to the future. This feature adds the specificity that coalitions can consist of an infinite number of agents. To be precise, it is the fact that a coalition can be formed by a countable infinity of agents that permits blocking allocations which would be impossible in an otherwise identical but finite economy. Specifically, coalitions formed by an infinite number of generations can reallocate their endowments in such a way that each generation gives a transfer when young and receives a transfer when old. By this process it might be possible to increase the income of some generations without decreasing the income of the rest of the members of the coalition. In other words, whereas the allocation of income in a finite economy is a zero sum game, this is not true for infinite-horizon, overlapping generations economies. The fact that these reallocations are feasible makes it possible to block consumption allocations which would belong to the core of the economy in a finite but otherwise identical model. This may serve as an explanation of why, as we shall demonstrate, Pareto optimal competitive equilibria might not belong to the core of an overlapping generations economy.

I.3. The Main Results

We start by carefully defining the bargaining problem faced by agents of a finite lifespan in an overlapping generations economy and justify why they behave as if coalitions with members of other generations were in fact possible. This leads us to model in Chapter V the problem of trust in intertemporal consumption allocations as a question of belonging or not to the core of the economy. We then provide a full characterization of the core allocations for n-goods pure exchange economies with one agent per generation : a consumption allocation belongs to the core if and only if is Pareto optimal and Time-wise Individually Rational (a temporary version of the notion of individual rationality).

This result has strong implications for models with one commodity per period. It is straightforward to realise that in these economies there is only one consumption allocation which is time-wise individually rational : the initial endowments. Thus, either the core is empty (when the initial endowments allocation is not Pareto optimal) or contains the initial endowments only. From this it follows that for one commodity economies no consumption allocation involving intertemporal transfers can belong to the core of the economy. In other words, no monetary equilibrium is socially viable. This result is no longer true for many goods models.

The existence problem is analysed for the many goods economy. In this respect we find that, for given aggregate endowments for every period, we can find specific individual allocations for which the core is non-empty, as well as alternative individual allocations for which the core is empty.

In Chapter VI we concentrate on the relation between competitive equilibria and the core of economies with many goods and one agent per generation. We find that all Pareto optimal Walrasian equilibria belong to the core. As for monetary equilibria we demonstrate that there exist bounds on the real value of equilibrium money purchases beyond which monetary equilibria are not socially viable. This result gives rigorous substance to the intuition that consumers might be willing to accept some amount of intrinsically worthless paper money, but not "too much".

For the many agents case, we distinguish between Walrasian, IOU and monetary equilibria. In the first kind of equilibrium every agent balances his budget in every period; in the second kind, generations as aggregates balance their budget every period, although some individual agents might not do so; and , finally, in the third kind of equilibria generations are net lenders when young and purchase outside, fiat money. Balasko and Shell [4] have demonstrated that all weakly Pareto optimal consumption allocations can be implemented as a Walrasian equilibrium after a suitable redistribution of the initial endowments. However, as we shall see, it is not true that every weakly Pareto optimal consumtion allocation can implemented as a monetary or as an IOU equilibrium for some appropriate redistribution of the initial endowments. In other words, there are some consumption allocations which can never be a non-walrasian competitive equilibrium irrespective of the distribution of endowments. In order to distinguish betwen the two kinds of consumption allocations, we define the "classical set" as the set of all the consumption allocations which can only be implemented as barter, Walrasian equilibria after any individual redistribution of initial endowments. We then demonstrate that all competitive allocations not belonging to the classical set either do not belong to the core or can become excluded from it after an appropriate redistribution of initial endowments within each generation. On the contrary, the competitive allocations in the classical set belong to the core for all the distributions of endowments for which it is a competitive equilibrium.

Since both monetary and IOU equilibria correspond to consumption allocations which by definition do not belong to the classical set, our results imply that they might not belong to the core. Further, we prove that as the economy is replicated all monetary equilibria become eventually excluded from the core.

I.4. The Core of Overlapping Generations Economies and the Theory of General Competitive Equilibrium

The Theory of General Competitive Equilibrium studies the properties of the competitive mechanism, i.e. the organization of economic activity by which agents make plans and trade in markets using exogenously given prices as the sole information and under the conjecture that no agent can affect such prices. Most of the contributions in this field have been obtained on the simplified model of an economy built by Arrow and Debreu. Thus it is relevant for the progress of our knowlegde of the competitive mechanism to verify the extent to which the fundamental results of competitive theory are robust with respect to the specification of the canonical Arrow-Debreu model.

Let us briefly recall the main results obtained for the Arrow-Debreu model. In the first place, the existence and determinacy of competitive equilibria is, of course, essential for the logical consistency of the model[3]. In the second place, we have the First Fundamental Theorem of Welfare Economics which says that the set of Walrasian allocations is a subset of the set of Pareto optimal allocations. This proves that competitive exchange through markets leads to efficient outcomes. Finally, the last result we wish

Figure I.1

Arrow-Debreu Economies

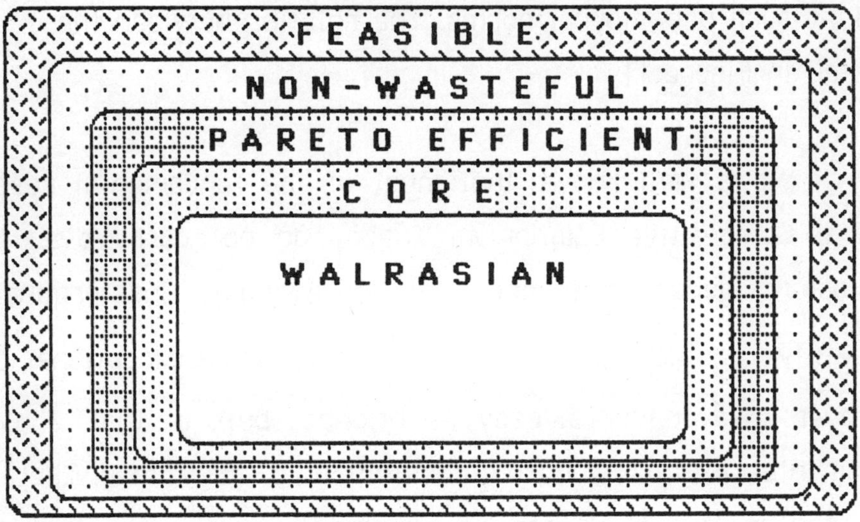

to mention is the important property of competitive allocations that they are a subset of the core of the economy and further that, as the economy is enlarged by replication, the core shrinks and at the limit coincides with the set of competitive equilibria.

This last result reinforces the plausibility of the competitive mechanism because it shows that agents could not have done better by by-passing the market and trying to reach direct deals with individuals or sub-groups of agents. Therefore, agents do rightly in behaving accordingly with the competitive conjecture. In other words, if competitive equilibria did not belong to the core it would be harder to justify that agents would stick to competitive behaviour in spite of the potential gains that could be obtained by breaking such behavioural norms. The relation between these sets is depicted in Figure I.1.

It is well known that most of the fundamental results in General Competitive Equilibrium Theory do not carry over to the overlapping generations model of an economy. Indeterminacy of competitive equilibria is the rule rather than the exceptional case[4]. Moreover, we have already mentioned before that the First Fundamental Welfare Theorem does not hold true either. The results contained in this book can be presented as showing that in the relationship between competitive equilibria and core the overlapping generations model departs again from the standard Arrow-Debreu model. Indeed, as we shall see, competitive equilibria are not a subset of the core of the economy. The relation between the different sets is depicted in Figure I.2. .

Figure I.2.

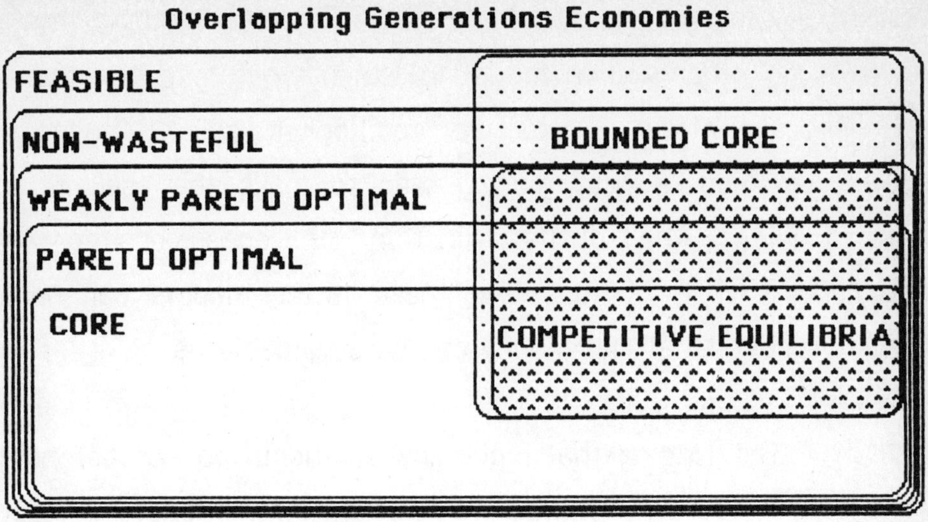

This departure with respect to the Arrow-Debreu model is deeper than might appear at first sight. Of course, none of the competitive equilibria failing to be Pareto efficient can belong to the core of the economy. But we find in Chapter VII that Pareto optimal competitive equilibria without fiat money might not belong to the core of the economy.[5] Therefore, as far as overlapping generations economies are concerned, the competitive mechanism not only can produce inefficient allocations but the competitive assumption itself might need further justification.

I.5. The Core of Overlapping Generations Economies and the Theory of Money

The overlapping generations model has been rapidly gaining ground as the most appropriate framework for the development of a theory of fiat money. This view has been forcefully argued by

Wallace [59] and Cass and Shell [13]. The fundamental point is that there is no other known model in which worthless fiat money can endogenously attain a positive equilibrium price. Other general equilibrium models with money need to make the assumption that money enters the utility function of consumers or similar assumptions. It is obvious that these latter models can hardly be used to "prove" that fiat money can be a valuable asset.

The finding that monetary equilibria do not belong to the core of the economy is thus of relevance for monetary theory . It may sound surprising that money is rejected by rational agents in an equilibrium in which it has positive value. But this is the essence of the argument. If one agents knows that money is a valuable good for future generations he has good reasons to reject existing money and introduce a new currency in the next period.

Let me stress that point by means of the following argument. It is common knowledge that monetary equilibria in overlapping generations models are like a Ponzi game : when entering one makes a down payment (in exchange for money) which is repaid by a newcomer when leaving the game. If asked to join a Ponzi game one could refuse on the grounds that this being a perfectly symmetrical zero sum game no agent could make any gain. This argument however heavily depends on the finiteness of the number of players. The fundamental point is that even if there were a countably infinite number of players one should still refuse entering a Ponzi game. The argument is as follows. If I am not confident of being able to introduce new players into the game I should not enter. But, if I am sure that I can bring new people into the game then I had better refuse joining the ongoing game and start a new one : I shall be paid without needing an entrance fee.

In order to see what goes wrong with monetary equilibria, let us first concentrate on the one commodity case. Monetary equilibria entail consumption allocations in which agents give some amount of the real good when young in exchange for a worthless piece of paper after having been persuaded that the next generation will in turn deliver real goods for that money. The essential point is the following. If I do not believe that the next period fiat money will actually exchange for real goods I would better off by not accepting the money I am offered today. But if was persuaded that money will have value tomorrow I would still be better off by refusing today's fiat money and create my own. Thus money is repudiated under all circumstances. The problem is more complex when there are many goods. In that case we shall have both intra-period and across-period exchanges. When blocking a monetary equilibrium the first member of the coalition gives up intra-period trading in the first period of his life for the sake of the expected gains from introducing new money in the second period. The larger the losses from renouncing to today's exchanges the harder an agent will find rejecting existing money. This is the source of the bounds on the amount of money purchases we have mentioned earlier. Thus blocking can be interpreted in the following way. Suppose that money served as a means of exchange (in the intra-period trading) as well as as a store of value (in the across-period trades). In the one commodity case, money was simply a pure store of value and in that case money was always refused. Thus , it is the role as a means of exchange what confers money social acceptability.

In Chapter VII we shall formally prove that even with many commodities monetary equilibria eventually become excluded from the core as the economy becomes large (by replication). Indeed the intra-period losses which agents belonging to a blocking coalition might incur are reduced as the number of agents per generation increases. In order to see that point more clearly, consider again the case of one agent per generation. Excluding agent t necessarily means that agent $t+1$ will not be able to trade when coexisting with agent t in period $t+1$. If agent t when old is endowed with an indispensible good, not possessed by agent $t+1$ when young, then agent $t+1$ will find it impossible to exclude agent t. However, this is no longer the case when there are two identical agents per generation. One of the two agents of generation t can be excluded without driving generation $t+1$ into starvation. They can trade with the other member of generation t. By this process the intra-period costs become smaller as the economy becomes large, and hence the result.

Summarizing, our results seem to give little hope for the use of overlapping generations models as an appropriate framework for monetary theory. For large economies monetary equilibria will not belong to the core thus making fiat money a socially unstable institution. In other words, and using the arguments examined in the previous section, for monetary equilibria the assumption that agents behave competitively would be lacking plausibility, unless we advocate the power of the state backing the contracts.

I.6. The "Social Contrivance of Money" Revisited

In our Chapter VII we obtain that as the economy is replicated no monetary equilibrium (with either outside or inside money) belongs to the core. This result may seem to be very negative for the body of monetary theory developed on the overlapping generations model. We think though that it can be given a positive interpretation which links quite naturally with Samuelson's view of money as a "social contrivance".

Indeed, in his original contribution Samuelson [50] was fully aware of the problem of the social acceptability of money. He made explicit that his analysis of the role of money was valid «as long as the new current generations of workers do not repudiate the old money» (p.481). This is the reason why he considered fiat money as a social contract. Because, «the Golden Rule of Kant's Categorical Imperative (enjoining like people to follow the common pattern that makes each best off) are often not self-enforcing: if all but one obey, the one may gain selfish advantage by disobeying -which is where the sheriff comes in: we politically invoke force on *ourselves*, attempting to make an unstable equilibrium a stable one» (p.480).

In spite of the fact that Samuelson clearly identified the problem, his idea of money as a "Hobbes-Rousseau" social contract has created some confusion. As Cass and Yaari [14] point out, the competitive conjecture simply rules out the possibility that agents not trust contracts. Indeed, whether or not it pays rational agents to obey a social rule needs an entirely different analytical framework: it is a topic that calls for a game theoretical approach.

The possibility that agents refuse existing money has been mentioned also by Shell [55] and Bryant [9] in association with the seigniorage produced by the creation of fiat money. Specifically, Shell's argument goes as follows: «Assume man 0 declares that the wrapper from his chocolate is money. If he is able to convince the future generation to accept his wrapper as legal tender, he will be able to make a chocolate profit called seigniorage. (...) The fragility of intergenerational social contracts shows up in our example. If the k-th generation repudiates the money of its elders, it can avoid passing chocolate backward. Furthermore, the k-th generation can gain seigniorage by printing new money. Under this monetary reform the reforming generation may have chocolate passed to it, but itself passes none backward» (pp.1006-1007). [6] Unfortunately, Shell did not pursue this line of thought any farther.

Our results can be interpreted as a rigorous analysis of the social acceptability of fiat money. Agents agree on the usefulness of fiat money but have conflict on the sharing of the seigniorage rights. As a matter of fact each generation tries to extract the full rights by refusing existing money. This strategic behaviour creates an innate instability for the monetary equilibria which can only be overcome by the force of the law: fiat money becomes "legal tender".[7] This solution simply confers the full seigniorage rights to the first generation. Therefore, from an institutional point of view, the results proven in the book can be interpreted as showing the need for paper money to be legal tender. And indeed our experience clearly is of a fiat money as a creature of the state and not as the outcome of a spontaneous agreement of economic agents.

Notes to Chapter I

1 In a similar fashion, the overlapping generations model with production has been used for the analysis of Social Security by Samuelson [51] and of Public Debt by Diamond [21]. In that case too it seems legitimate to ask whether these social institutions would be found acceptable by all participating agents. Adam Smith reports in his *Wealth of Nations* (Book V Chap.II) that the government of Pennsylvania had to declare legal tender his public debt in order to grant its acceptability.

From a more theoretical point of view, for Diamond's [21] analysis of public debt to work it is essential that private shares and public debt are seen by consumers as perfect substitutes in the stock market. It is doubful that rational consumers would not take into account the fact that, in contrast with shares on real assets, public debt is a financial instrument with no intrinsic value.

2 The non-cooperative approach has been used by Shubik [56] and [57, Ch.16] who analyses a game of division of "income" among the three generations coexisting in every period.

3 As analysed by Debreu [20].

4 See for instance Kehoe and Levine [42].

5 D. Kovenock [43] has provided another example of a Pareto optimal competitive allocation not in the core.

6 Bryant [9] refers to the observation by Shell on the problem of seigniorage and considers it to be «a problem which must be addressed by any model of valued fiat money» (p.236). Indeed, Bryant points out that «in a model with costless contracts this seigniorage problem can arise if there are a countably infinite number of individuals. There is no Nash equilibrium set of contracts in such a model.»

[7] The traditional views on the importance of the legal backing of fiat money have never been unanimous. As a minor illustration we can contrast the views of Fisher and Wicksteed. Irving Fisher in his *Elementary Principles of Economics* , 1910, defines the nature of money in the following way: «We define money as *goods generally acceptable in exchange for other goods* . The facility with which it may thus be exchanged, or its general acceptability, is the chief characteristic of money. The general acceptability may be reënforced (sic) by law, the money thus becoming "legal tender" (i.e., money which may be legally tendered or offered by a debtor to his creditor as a means of discharging his obligations expressed in terms of money units and which the creditor must accept). But such reënforcement is not essential. All that is necessary in order that any good may be money is that general acceptability shall attach to it» (p.147). This view is in sharp contrast with the opinions held by his contemporary P.H. Wicksteed in *The Common Sense of Political Economy*, 1910 for whom the acceptability of paper money is chiefly due to the power of the government to enforce it by law (pp.618-619).

PART II

The Overlapping Generations Model of an Exchange Economy

The purpose of this Part II is to provide a simple introduction to the Overlapping Generations model of pure exchange economies. We shall concentrate on the essential theoretical problems and leave aside the applied implications. Besides describing the basic model, we shall study the appropriate characterization of efficiency in an infinite horizon, dynamic framework. This is done in Chapter II. We shall later deal with intertemporal consumer behaviour and examine the competitive equilibria of the model, its existence and uniqueness. This is the object of Chapter III. Finally, in Chapter IV we shall discuss the role of money in the economy and its effect on consumer behaviour. We shall then show that there exist monetary equilibria in the sense that there are competitive equilibria in which worthless fiat money can attain a positive market price.

Most of the literature in the area has been developed around the one good model. There are good reasons for this simplifying assumption. After all, in an Overlapping Generations model one attempts to capture the essence of the intertemporal allocation process. It seems thus justifiable to focus on the inter-period allocation of lifetime income and leave aside the intra-period problem of allocating that expenditure among the different goods.

For most of this Part II the Overlapping Generations model will be developed in the simplified one-commodity world. This will help to make the essential arguments simpler, without going into technical discussions which may obscure the main issues. Nevertheless, each chapter contains one section discussing the extention of the basic results to the n-goods case.

The aim of this Part II is merely expositional. Virtually all the results presented here are well known, eventhough in some cases the method of proof is original. The style we have used here is rigurous and sometimes technical, but we have avoided formality in order to make the exposition lighter.

Chapter II Dynamic Efficiency

II.1. The structure of the basic model

We shall consider that time is measured in discrete intervals of one unit length[1] and that the economy extends itself over an infinite sequence of such elementary time periods, t= 1, 2, 3, ...

In each period one "generation" of consumers is born and lives for two periods. We can thus meaningfully speak of the "youth" ant the "old age" of a consumer. We shall use the birthdate to identify each generation. At any given period t two generations will be alive: the one just born (generation t) and the one born in the previous period (generation $t-1$), which will then be in its old age. It is the essence of Overlapping Generation models that the exchange may take place between agents at different stages of their lifecycle. For most of this Part II we shall assume that each generation is composed of one agent only, but we shall always include a section extending the results to economies with many commodities. Therefore, with one commodity per period and one agent per generation, any exchange will have to be intergenerational. At the beginning of this economy there exists a generation previously born at time $t=0$.

In order to keep the model simple and comprehensible we shall assume that there is only one perishable commodity in every period. We shall denote by $c^t(t+s)$ the consumption of that commodity by agent t at period $t+s$, $s=0,1$, by $c^t \in \mathbb{R}^2_+$ the consumption of agent t in the two periods he is alive, i.e. $c^t=(c^t(t),c^t(t+1))$. Since generation

0 will be alive for the period $t=1$ only, his consumption will simply be $c^0=c^0(1)$. A consumption allocation is a sequence c specifying the consumption assigned to each consumer in every period t, i.e. $c = \{c^0, c^1, c^2, \dots\}$.

We shall let $w^t(t+s)$ denote the initial endowment of agent t of the good available at period $t+s$, $s=0,1$, and $w^t \in \mathbb{R}^2_+$ the vector of endowments corresponding to the two periods that the agent will be alive. Again, for generation $t=0$ we have that $w^0=w^0(1)$. Aggregate endowments at period t will be denoted by $w(t)$, i.e. $w(t) = w^{t-1}(t)+w^t(t)$. Finally, we shall let w be the sequence $w=\{w^0, w^1, w^2, \dots\}$. The sequence of individual endowments will be assumed to be uniformly bounded from below and from above.

Preferences of consumer t can be represented by a utility function $u^t:\mathbb{R}^2_+ \rightarrow \mathbb{R}$, for $t=1,2,\dots$ and $u^0:\mathbb{R}_+ \rightarrow \mathbb{R}$, for $t=0$. We shall assume that u^t is differentiable strictly increasing and strictly quasi-concave.

II.2. Intertemporal Efficiency

In spite of its simplicity, we are allowing for preferences to experience ample variation from generation to generation. In order to obtain positive results we shall need to restrict the set of admissible preferences. The essential assumption will fall on the range of values that the marginal rate of intertemporal substitution can take.

In a model where consumers make intertemporal choices the marginal rate of intertemporal substitution is bound to play a crucial role. It tells us how much we shall have to be compensated in tomorrow's good for giving up one unit of today's consumption good. With one commodity per period the marginal rate of intertemporal substitution, $MRS^t(c^t)$ can be written as

$$\frac{d\, c^t(t+1)}{d\, c^t(t)} = \frac{\partial u^t(c^t)/\partial c^t(t)}{\partial u^t(c^t)/\partial c^t(t+1)} \equiv MRS^t(c^t) \cdot$$

Our assumption on preferences is that there exist k and K, with $0<k<1$ and $K>0$, such that there exist $c, \tilde{c} \in C$ for which

(II.2) $$MRS^t(c^t) \leqq 1-k \quad \text{and} \quad MRS^t(\tilde{c}^t) \geqq 1+K \quad \text{for } t=1,2,\ldots \;.$$

This assumption is quite mild. Bearing in mind that we can find in the set C consumption allocation sequences giving all the available consumption when agents are young and nothing when they are old, or the other way around, our assumption simply says that the marginal rate of intertemporal substitution will vary sufficiently between these extreme allocations.

The standard notion of efficiency is the one proposed by Pareto according to which a consumption allocation will be considered efficient if there is no feasible reallocation of the individual consumption assignments that makes somebody better off and nobody worse off. In a dynamic model as the one laid down in the previous section these reallocations typically take place among individuals belonging to two consecutive generations. In the that case the reallocation will take the form of a transfer of goods between a young agent and an old agent in a given period.

The fact that in Overlapping Generations models there are infinite agents (a countable infinity, to be precise) has important implications for our understanding of efficiency. In order to make this point sharper we shall contrast the overlapping generations model with an otherwise identical model but for the fact that the latter will have a finite number of consumers.

Let us therefore consider an economy with agents up to generation T and hence with T+1 agents, that is, t=0,1,2,...,T. We shall call such an economy a T-economy[2]. It should be kept in mind that in our T-economy there will be two agents alive in every period for the first T periods, but that generation T will still be alive an additional period on his own.

Aggregate endowments available at each date t will be denoted by $\overline{w}(t)$. A consumption allocation c will be feasible for a T-economy if it satisfies

$$\text{(II.1)} \qquad c^t(t) + c^{t-1}(t) \leq \overline{w}(t)\,, \; t=1,2,\ldots,T\,, \text{ and}$$

$$c^T(T+1) \leq \overline{w}^T(T+1)\,.$$

Let us denote by C(T) the set of all feasible consumption allocation sequences.

We can now state the first result fully characterising the Pareto efficent consumption allocations for a T-economy.

Proposition II.1 For a T-economy with one good per period a consumption allocation c is Pareto optimal if and only if

(II.3) $$c^t(t) + c^{t-1}(t) = \bar{w}(t)\ ,\ t=1,2,\ \ldots,\ T\ ,\ \text{and}$$
$$c^T(T+1) = \bar{w}^T(T+1).$$

Proof.- Assume that the consumption allocation c is feasible but does not satisfy (II.3), that is, for some period r we have that

$$c^r(r) + c^{r-1}(r) < \bar{w}(r).$$

We can then construct a new consumption allocation $\tilde{c}$ which dominates c. Simply consider $\tilde{c}$ equal to c except for $\tilde{c}^r(r)$, where $\tilde{c}^r(r) = \bar{w}(r) - c^{r-1}(r)$. It is immediate that all agent will have as much utility under $\tilde{c}$ than under c , except for agent r who is going to be strictly better off. This proves necessity.

Let us prove sufficiency by contradiction. Therefore, let us assume that c satisfies (II.3) but is not Pareto optimal, i.e. that there exists a feasible consumption allocation $\tilde{c}$ that Pareto dominates c. Let us assume that consumer r is strictly better off.

First of all note that $\tilde{c}^t(t)+\tilde{c}^{t-1}(t)=c^t(t)+c^{t-1}(t)=\overline{w}(t)$, $t=1,2,...T$, and $\tilde{c}^T(T+1)=c^T(T+1)=\overline{w}^T(T+1)$. Since for agent $t=0$ $u^0(\tilde{c}^0(1))\geqq u^0(c^0(1))$, we have that $\tilde{c}^0(1)\geqq c^0(1)$. By feasibility at $t=1$ we have that $\tilde{c}^1(1)\leqq c^1(1)$. By repeatedly applying this argument we shall have that $\tilde{c}^t(t)<c^t(t)$ for $t=r+1, r+2,..., T$. But by feasiblity $\tilde{c}^T(T+1)=c^T(T+1)=\overline{w}^T(T+1)$. Therefore

$$u^T(\tilde{c}^T(T),\tilde{c}^T(T+1))<u^T(c^T(T),c^T(T+1))$$

and this contradicts the assumption that $\tilde{c}$ Pareto dominates c. QED

It is obvious that Proposition II.1 holds true irrespective of the value of T. Observe now that the Overlapping Generations model corresponds to the case in which T has become infinity. However, in spite of the fact that the Overlapping Generations model is the limit of the sequence of T-economies as T tends to infinity, Proposition II.1 does not hold true for the limit economy. In other words, we shall now demonstrate that condition (II.3) is not sufficient for dynamic, infinite horizon efficiency in Overlapping Generations economies.

Proposition II.2 In an Overlapping Generations Economy with preferences satisfying (II.2) and one good per period we can find consumption allocations satisfying (II.3) that are not Pareto efficient.

Proof.- Let us start by considering the sequences $x(t)$, such that

(II.4) $$0 \leq x(t) \leq \bar{w}(t) \text{ for } t=1,2,\dots \; .$$

Let us denote by X the set of sequences x satisfying (II.4). It is essential to note that we can generate all the consumption allocation sequences satisfying (II.3) by choosing $c^t(t)=x(t)$ and $c^{t-1}(t)=\bar{w}(t)-x(t)$, $t=1,2,\dots$, for all $x \in X$.

In order to prove Proposition II.2 we need to show that we can find $x, \hat{x} \in X$ such that

(II.5) $$u^t(x(t), \bar{w}(t+1)-x(t+1)) - u^t(\hat{x}(t), \bar{w}(t+1)-\hat{x}(t+1)) \geqq 0,$$
$$t=1,2,\dots, \quad \text{and} \quad u^0(\bar{w}(1)-x(1))-u^0(\bar{w}(1)-\hat{x}(1)) \geqq 0.$$

By the strict quasi-concavity of u^t we have the following inequalities

$$[x(t)-\hat{x}(t)]\partial u^t(x^t)/\partial c^t(t) + [\hat{x}(t+1)-x(t+1)]\partial u^t(x^t)/\partial c^t(t+1) \leqq$$
(II.6) $$\leqq u^t(x(t), \bar{w}(t+1)-x(t+1)) - u^t(\hat{x}(t), \bar{w}(t+1)-\hat{x}(t+1)) \leqq$$
$$\leqq [x(t)-\hat{x}(t)]\partial u^t(\hat{x}^t)/\partial c^t(t)+[\hat{x}(t+1)-x(t+1)]\partial u^t(\hat{x}^t)/\partial c^t(t+1)$$
$$\text{for } t=1,2,3,\dots \; .$$

Consider now the sequences x and $\hat{x}$ such that $\hat{x}(t)-$

$x(t)=s>0$ for $t=1,2,3,\ldots$. Substituting into (II.6) and manipulating we obtain

$$s(1-MRS^{t}(x))\,\partial u^{t}(x^{t})/\partial c^{t}(t+1)\leqq$$

$$\text{(II.7)}\qquad \leqq u^{t}(x(t),\,\overline{w}(t+1)-x(t+1)) - u^{t}(\breve{x}(t),\,\overline{w}(t+1)-\breve{x}(t+1) \leqq$$

$$\leqq s(1-MRS^{t}(\breve{x}))\,\partial u^{t}(\breve{x}^{t})/\partial c^{t}(t+1).$$

Therefore by chosing x and $\breve{x}$ such that $\breve{x}(t)-x(t)=s>0$ and such that $MRS^{t}(x)\leqq 1$, accordingly with (II.7) the consumption allocation sequence generated by the sequence x Pareto dominates the consumption allocation generated by $\breve{x}$ and hence that consumption allocation is not Pareto optimal. Observe, finally, that $u^{0}(x(1))>u^{0}(\breve{x}(1))$. Since individual preferences have been assumed to satisfy (II.2), such pair of sequences x and $\breve{x}$ do exist. QED.

We have thus seen that for infinite horizon Overlapping Generations economies consumption allocations satisfying (II.3) may be inefficient. Eventhough (II.3) is not sufficient to distinguish between efficient and inefficient consumption allocations, it can be useful in classifying inefficient allocations. Indeed, in spite of the fact that they are not fully efficient, it is obvious that a consumption allocation satisfying (II.3) is "less inefficient" than one that does not even satisfy it. It seems thus useful to introduce a weaker notion of dynamic efficiency that takes this problem into account. On this point, observe first that the discussion of efficiency in T-economies is formaly identical to performing the same exercise in an Overlapping

Generations economy in which we allow the sequences c and $\tilde{c}$ to differ for the first T periods of time. We can thus say that a consumption allocation sequence c is "short run Pareto optimal" or "weakly Pareto optimal" if there is no feasible consumption allocation $\tilde{c}$ which differs from c on a finite number of periods and Pareto dominates c.[3]

We have proven in Proposition II.2 that there may exist consumption allocation sequences that are "weakly" efficient but not Pareto efficient. It seems now useful to provide criteria for distinguishing weakly from dynamically efficient sequences.

Let us consider a weakly efficient consumption allocation c. In order to verify whether or not c is Pareto optimal we have to check whether we can find another consumption allocation $\tilde{c}$ that Pareto dominates c . From Proposition II.1 we know that if such a sequence $\tilde{c}$ does exist it will have to differ from c on an infinite number of periods. The following result will tell us about the sign of this difference.

Lemma II.1 Let c be a weakly efficient consumption allocation sequence. A necessary condition for $\tilde{c}$ to Pareto dominate c is that there exists t_0 such that $\tilde{c}^{t-1}(t)>c^{t-1}(t)$, $t \geqq t_0$.

Proof.- Let t_0 be the first agent with a strict utility gain under $\tilde{c}$. It can be readily verified that $c^t = \tilde{c}^t$ for $t = 0,1,2,\dots,t_0 - 1$ and that $\tilde{c}^{t_0}(t_0+1) < c^{t_0}(t_0+1)$, because feasibility at period t_0 requires that $c^{t_0}(t_0) = \tilde{c}^{t_0}(t_0)$. By repeatedly applying the same argument and bearing in mind that u^t is strictly increasing in the two arguments we can obtain the desired result. Observe that if the sequences x and $\tilde{x}$ generate the consumption sequences c and $\tilde{c}$, respectively, Lemma II.1 implies that $x(t)>\tilde{x}(t)$, $t \geq t_0+1$. QED.

We can now provide sufficient condition for a consumption allocation sequence be Pareto optimal. This condition simply requires that the marginal rate of intertemporal substitution be greater than unity after some generation.

Proposition II.3 Let c be a weakly efficient consumption allocation sequence such that

(II.8) $$\operatorname{Lim\,inf}_{t\to\infty} MRS^t(c^t)>1.$$

Then c is Pareto optimal.

Proof.- Suppose not, i.e. that condition (II.8) is satisfied but that c is not Pareto optimal. Therefore, there must exist a feasible consumption allocation $\tilde{c}$ that Pareto dominates c. Let t_0 be the first agent with a strict utility gain under $\tilde{c}$. From Lemma II.1 we know that $x(t)>\tilde{x}(t)$, $t \geq t_0+1$. Further, because of strict quasi-concavity of u^t, inequality (II.6) holds strictly for $t \geq t_0+1$. Therefore, we can obtain from (II.6) by rearranging terms that

$$(II.9)\quad \partial u^t(c^t)/\partial c^t(t+1)\{[x(t)-\tilde{x}(t)]MRS^{\,t}(x(t),\bar{w}(t+1)-x(t+1))+\tilde{x}(t+1)-x(t+1)\}<u^{\,t}(x(t),\bar{w}(t+1)-x(t+1))-u^{\,t}(\tilde{x}(t),\bar{w}(t+1)-\tilde{x}(t+1)).$$

For any Pareto dominating sequence $\tilde{x}$, we have that

$$u^t(x(t),\bar{w}(t+1)-x(t+1))-u^{\,t}(\tilde{x}(t),\bar{w}(t+1)-\tilde{x}(t+1) < 0, \text{ for } t\geqq t_0+1.$$

Taking into account that $\partial u^t(c^t)/\partial c^t(t+1)>0$, we have that a necessary condition for any $\tilde{c}$ that Pareto dominates c is that

$$(II.10)\qquad [x(t)-\tilde{x}(t)]MRS^t(x(t),\bar{w}(t+1)-x(t+1))<[x(t+1)-\tilde{x}(t+1)],\quad \text{for } t\geqq t_0+1.$$

By Lemma II.1 $x(t)-\tilde{x}(t)>0$. Therefore, if

$$\text{Lim inf}_{t\to\infty} MRS^t(x(t),\bar{w}(t+1)-x(t+1))>1,$$

any sequence $\tilde{x}$ Pareto dominating x and satisfying (II.10) will eventually become unfeasible. QED.

Let us now provide a stronger version of the previous result [4]. The interest of the new condition is that it can be easily interpreted in terms of the associated supporting prices.

Lemma II.2 Let c be a weakly efficient consumption allocation sequence such that

$$(II.11)\qquad \text{Lim}_{t\to\infty} \Pi^t{}_{r=1} MRS^r(c^r)=+\infty.$$

Then c is Pareto optimal.

Proof.- By compounding inequality (II.10) we obtain that

$$\text{(II.12)} \qquad [x(1)-\bar{x}(1)]\Pi^{t}_{r=t_0} MRS^{t}(x(t),\bar{w}(t+1)-x(t+1))< [x(t+1)-\bar{x}(t+1)], \quad \text{for } t\geq t_0+1,$$

is a necessary condition for $\bar{x}$ to Pareto dominate x. It is immediate that under condition (II.11) there is no $\bar{x}$ satisfying (II.12). QED.

Let us denote by $p(t)$ the supporting prices of good t and by p the sequence $p=\{p(1),p(2),p(3),....\}$. We shall normalize by chosing $p(1)=1$. If p is the sequence of prices supporting the weakly efficient consumption allocation sequence c, we have that

$$MRS^{t}(c^{t})=p(t)/p(t+1).$$

We can now state the following Proposition[5].

Proposition II.4 Let c be a weakly efficient consumption allocation sequence with supporting prices p such that

$$\text{(II.13)} \qquad \mathrm{Lim}_{t\rightarrow\infty}\, p(t)=0.$$

Then c is Pareto optimal.

Proof.- The result immediately follows from Lemma II.2 and the observation that

$$\Pi^t_{r=1} MRS^r(c^r) = p(1)/p(t+1). \text{ QED.}$$

Proposition II.4 is but a restatement of the well known "golden rule" theorem for dynamic efficiency. It simply says that the interest rate should not be lower than the growth rate.

Balasko and Shell [4] have provided a complete characterization of Pareto optimal consumption allocation sequences. Since we do not wish to become too technical, we shall state their result without going into the details of the formal proof. Intuition about this result will be provided later in the discussion of its generalization to many commodities.

Proposition II.5 The weakly efficient consumption allocation sequence with supporting prices p is Pareto efficient if and only if

(II.14) $$\Sigma\, 1/p(t) = +\infty .$$

Proof.- See Balasko and Shell[6].

II.3 Intertemporal Efficiency with Many Commodities

After examining the essentials of the Overlapping Generations model in its simplest specification, we shall complete the analysis by studying the specific problems that arise in a many commodity world. This extension includes not only the obvious generalization to economies with a large number of commodities in each period but, as shown by Balasko and Shell (1981), to the case of multiperiod lifes, which can be relabeled as an increase in the number of commodities.

Let us first adapt our notation to the n-commodity case. We shall denote by $c^t(t+s,i)$ the consumption of commodity i by agent t at period $t+s$, $s=0,1$, $i=1,\dots,n$, by $c^t \in \mathbb{R}^{2n}_+$ the consumption of agent t in the two periods he is alive, i.e. $c^t=(c^t(t),c^t(t+1))$. Since generation 0 will be alive for the period $t=1$ only, his consumption will simply be $c^0=c^0(1)$. A consumption allocation is a sequence c specifying the consumption assigned to each consumer in every period t, i.e. $c = \{c^0, c^1, c^2, \dots\}$.

We shall let $w^t(t+s,i)$ denote the initial endowment of agent t of the good i available at period $t+s$, $s=0,1$, $i=1,\dots,n$, and $w^t \in \mathbb{R}^{2n}_+$ the vector of endowments corresponding to the two periods that the agent will be alive. Again, for generation $t=0$ we have that $w^0=w^0(1)$. Aggregate endowments at period t will be denoted by $w(t)$, that is $w(t)=w^{t-1}(t)+w^t(t)$. Finally, we shall let w be the sequence $w=\{w^0, w^1, w^2, \dots\}$. The sequence of individual endowments will be assumed to be uniformly bounded from below away from zero and from above.

Preferences of consumer t can be represented by a utility function $u^t:\mathbb{R}^{2n}_+ \to \mathbb{R}$, for t=1,2,... and $u^0: \mathbb{R}^n_+ \to \mathbb{R}$, for t=0. We shall assume that u^t is twice differentiable, strictly increasing and strictly quasi-concave. Further, we shall assume that the first derivatives are uniformly bounded below away from zero and above for every consumption sequence which itself is uniformly bounded below away from zero and above.

In section II.2 we have introduced the notions of weak Pareto optimality and Pareto optimality in order to capture the difference between short-run efficiency and dynamic, intertemporal efficiency. The same definitions are valid for the more general case of many commodities. For weak Pareto optimality we require the consumption allocation not be Pareto dominated by any feasible reallocation over a finite number of periods. Pareto optimality of a consumption allocation implies that it not be dominated by any other feasible allocation even if differs from the first one over an infinite number of periods.

Proposition II.1 gives a full characterization of weakly Pareto optimal allocations for economies with one commodity per period. This characterization amounts to a full use of available resources. For the many commodity case this condition is necessary but not sufficient. The following Proposition extends the result mentioned to economies wit many commodities.

Proposition II.6 A consumption allocation sequence c is weakly Pareto optimal if and only if

i) $c^{t-1}(t)+c^t(t)=w^{t-1}(t)+w^t(t)$, and

ii) $$\frac{\partial u^{t-1}/\partial c^{t-1}(t,i)}{\partial u^{t-1}/\partial c^{t-1}(t,j)} = \frac{\partial u^{t}/\partial c^{t}(t,i)}{\partial u^{t}/\partial c^{t}(t,j)}, \quad i,j=1,\ldots,n, \quad t=1,2,\ldots$$

<u>Proof</u>.- Observe first that i) is a necessary condition for weak efficiency. If we had strict inequality for some period t^0, by the assumption that utility functions are strictly increasing, it would be possible to increase the utility of any of the two agents living at t^0 without changing the remaining elements of the consumption sequence. We would need only assigning the iddle resources to any of the two agents or both. Therefore, that consumption allocation would not be weakly Pareto optimal. We shall thus assume for the rest of the proof the i) is satisfied.

Let us now consider the sets $C^{t-1}(t)$ and $C^{t}(t)$ as defined by

$$C^{t-1}(t)=\{(c^{t-1}(t-1),\tilde{c}^{t-1}(t))/\ u^{t-1}(c^{t-1}(t-1),\tilde{c}^{t-1}(t))\geq u^{t-1}(c^{t-1})\}$$

and

$$C^{t}(t)=\{(\tilde{c}^{t}(t),c^{t}(t+1))/\ u^{t}(\tilde{c}^{t}(t),c^{t}(t+1))\geq u^{t}(c^{t})\}.$$

Condition ii) implies that these two sets are tangent. Hence, since i) is satisfied, it is not possible to reallocate the available resources over a finite number of periods so as to increase the utility of one agent without diminishing the utility of someone else. Hence, if a consumption allocation c satisfies i) and ii), then it is weakly Pareto optimal.

Conversely, it is immediate that if a consumption allocation sequence is weakly Pareto optimal it must satisfy i). The fact that c is weakly Pareto optimal implies that the sets $C^{t-1}(t)$ and $C^t(t)$ are tangent and can be separated by a hyperplane tangent to the two sets. If this were not true, the allocations in the intersection of the two sets would dominate the initial one. The differentiability of the utility functions together with the tangency of the sets $C^{t-1}(t)$ and $C^t(t)$ imply that condition ii) has to be satisfied. QED.

In order to illustrate the distinction between the two concepts we shall use Figure II.1, in which consumption allocations are depicted as points in a sequence of Edgeworth boxes. For this representation to be legitimate we need to assume intertemporal separability of individual preferences. This assumption implies that for every agent the indifference curves in every period are invariant to the consumption allocation corresponding to the other period. In this case the set of weakly Pareto optimal consumption allocations is given by all the sequences formed by taking points on the contract curve of every Edgeworth box. Thus weak Pareto optimality implies that the consumption allocation is efficient in every period taken independently. But while weak Pareto optimality is a necessary condition for Pareto optimality, it is by no means sufficient. Consider, for instance, the case of preferences satisfying

$$g^t(v^t_t(0),v^t_{t+1}(c^t(t+1)))= g^t(v^t_t(c^t(t)),v^t_{t+1}(0))=0$$

with $u^t(c^t)>0$ for all $c^t \in \mathbb{R}^{2n}_{++}$. Let us consider the consumption allocation c with $c^t=(0,c^t(t+1))$, for $t=1,2,\ldots$, corresponding to points A(t) and A(t+1) in Figure II.1 . This consumption allocation is weakly Pareto optimal because the sequence of points A belong to the

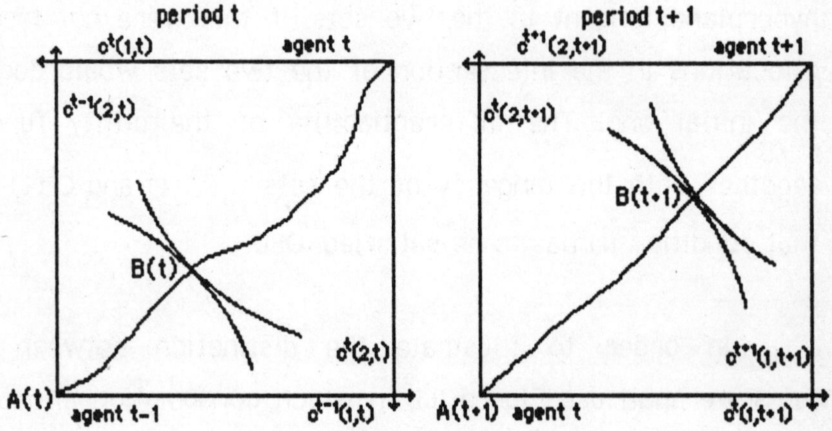

Figure II.1

contract curve in every period. Yet, this consumption allocation is not Pareto optimal because any other weakly Pareto optimal allocation belonging to the interior of the Edgeworth boxes will be preferable for every agent. This is the case of points B as depicted in Figure II.1.

From Proposition II.6 it is obvious that the marginal rates of intraperiod good substitution can be interpreted as relative (supporting) prices. Hence, with many commodities per period too one can easily obtain an equivalent of the Second Welfare Theorem for weakly Pareto optimal allocations. This would be a generalization of Proposition II.12.

We have shown in earlier sections that in Overlapping Generations economies the set of Pareto optimal allocations is a strict subset of the set of weakly Pareto optimal allocations. Therefore, and at variance with the standard Arrow-Debreu model, the fact that one can associate supporting prices to an allocation does not imply that it is Pareto optimal.

In section II.2 we have proven three Propositions giving price characterizations for Pareto optimal consumption allocations. The strongest result is the necessary and sufficient condition introduced in Proposition II.5 according to which the critical test consists in checking for the convergence of the sum of the inverse of prices. Then we provided some intuition for the weaker result proven as Proposition II.4. We shall now restate Proposition II.5 for the case of n commodities. This result has been proven by Balasko and Shell (1980) and Okuno and Zilcha (1980), both elaborating on the fundamental ideas about intertemporal efficiency laid down by Cass (1972). In stead of repeating the proof we shall provide an informal, but technical, intuition for this result.

Let p be the sequence of supporting prices of a given weakly Pareto optimal consumption allocation c, $p=\{p(1), p(2),...,p(t),...\}$, where $p(t)\in\mathbb{R}^n_{++}$, and $p(t,i)$ is the price of commodity i at period t. Let now y be the sequence of "incomes", $y=\{y^1, y^2,...\}$, associated with a given weakly Pareto optimal consumption sequence c and its corresponding supporting prices p, such that $y^t=p(t)c^t(t)+p(t+1)c^t(t+1)$, $t=1,2,...$. y^t is the value of the consumption allocation c^t evaluated at the supporting prices and both supporting prices and incomes are defined up to a positive scalar at the individual level. Once we consider the full economy all but one of these degrees of freedom are used up by the requirement that the supporting prices faced by different consumers for the same commodities must be identical. We can use the one degree of freedom we have been left with by arbitrarily fixing $p(1,1)=1$. Thus supporting prices and incomes will be normalized in terms of units of good 1 at period 1.

The following maximization problem is now well defined :

$$\text{Max } u^t(c^t) \text{ subject to } p(t)c^t(t)+p(t+1)c^t(t+1)\leqq y^t.$$

The first order conditions yield

(II.15) $$\partial u^t/\partial c^t(t+s,i) = \lambda^t p(t+s,i) \quad , \; s=0,1, \; i=1,\ldots,n, \; t=1,2,\ldots \; .$$

We can now proceed to the formal statement of the fundamental characterization theorem for Pareto optimal consumption allocations.

Proposition II.7 A weakly Pareto optimal consumption allocation sequence c is Pareto optimal if and only if

(II.16) $$\Sigma 1/\|p(t)\| = +\infty.$$

Proof.- See, for instance, Balasko and Shell (1980).

Let us now give an intuition and an original sketch of a proof for Proposition II.7. Let us consider the aggregate utility fall produced by a decrease of ϵ to every individual of the economy. This operation would freed an infinite amount of aggregate income. The aggregate utility fall as $\epsilon \to 0$ is given by $-\Sigma\lambda^t$. Using the first order conditions we can substitute every λ^t by the ratio of the marginal utility of that agent with respect to any good and the supporting price of that good. However, in order to keep our analysis close to the result given in Proposition II.7, we shall use the following equality that can be easily derived from (II.15),

(II.17) $$\| \partial u^t/\partial c^t(t) \| = \lambda^t \; \| p(t) \| \quad .$$

Therefore, the total utility loss can be rewritten as

(II.18) $$-\Sigma\lambda^t = -\Sigma \| \partial u^t/\partial c^t(t) \| / \| p(t) \| \; .$$

From the assumption about the uniform boundedness of the first derivatives of the utility functions, it follows that there exist k and K such that $k \leqq \| \partial u^t/\partial c^t(t) \| \leqq K$. Hence

(II.19) $$-K\, \Sigma 1/\| p(t) \| \leqq -\Sigma\lambda^t \leqq -k\, \Sigma 1/\| p(t) \| \; .$$

If the aggregate utility loss is finite, by the continuity of the first derivatives of the utility function, it would still be finite for small ϵ. Saving an infinite amount of income would have produced a finite fall in the aggregate utility. In that case the original allocation is not efficient. Conversely, when the utility fall is unbounded, there is no way of reallocating the income and compensate the loosers and hence that allocation will be Pareto optimal. In view of (II.19) it is immediate that $\Sigma\, \lambda^t$ diverges if and only if $\Sigma 1/\|p(t)\|$ diverges. In other words, a consumption allocation is Pareto optimal if and only if (II.16) in Proposition II.7 is satisfied.

Notes to Chapter II

1 Working with continuous time makes the analysis technically harder and does not seem to add any new insight. The only Overlapping Generations model with contionuous time that I know is the one due to Cass and Yaari [15].

2 Note that a T-economy can be reinterpreted as an Arrow-Debreu economy. Consider that the commodity space is $\mathbb{R}_+^{T+1}$. Individual preferences can be represented by u^t: $\mathbb{R}_+^{T+1} \rightarrow \mathbb{R}$. The index t used to identify consumers can be reinterpreted as refering to the type of preferences that correspond to this consumer. Therefore, consumers of type t while having preferences defined over the entire commodity space, his utility would be strictly increasing on its t-th and t+1-th arguments only.

3 The notion of "short run Pareto optimality" was first introduced by Balasko and Shell [4], who also use the alternative expression of "weak Pareto optimality".

4 In order to see that the result stated in Lemma II.2 is stronger than the one given in Proposition II.3, consider the case in which $MRS^t(c^t) = 0.9$ for t odd and $MRS^t(c^t)=1.2$ for t even. The Lim inf of that sequence is 0.9, which clearly does not satisfy Proposition II.3, but it does for Lemma II.2.

5 This result has been proven by Balasko and Shell[4] and Okuno and Zilcha[47].

6 This result was also proven by Okuno and Zilcha [47]. Balasko and Shell [4] require the following additional technical assumptions:

i) consumption sequences are uniformly bounded below;

ii) Marginal rates of substitution are uniformly bounded below and above; and

iii) the curvature of indifference surfaces (as measured

Gauss' index) is uniformly bounded above and below. Note however that as proven by Burke [10] the boundedness of the Gaussian curvature is not really needed. We shall discuss further this topic later in section II.3.

Chapter III <u>Competitive Equilibria in a Barter, Overlapping Generations Economy</u>

III.1. <u>Consumer Behaviour</u>

Consumers seek to maximise their utility under the constraints imposed by their own resources and the available markets. The fact that some markets might not be in operation would have to be taken into account by consumers when making their choices. For the time being we shall assume that the market structure is complete and therefore that spot and future markets operate at each date. In an Arrow-Debreu economy, the existence of a complete set of spot and future markets implies that all transactions take place at the begining of the economy. In the subsequent periods agents simply deliver and collect the goods they contracted for. However, in Overlapping Generations economies, the fact that in every period there are new consumers entering the economy induces a completely different picture. For markets will have to reopen and new trades will take place at each date.

We shall restrict our analysis to rational expectation, self-fulfilling equilibria. Therefore we shall not need to distinguish between expected and realized prices. We shall denote by $p(t)$ the price of commodity delivered at period t and by p the price sequence $p=\{p(1), p(2),...\}$.

We shall assume that consumers behave competitively, i.e. that in making their choices they disregard everybody else's actions and seek to maximise their own objective function under the believe that at the exogenously given prices he can actually sell or purchase any desired amount.

Let us start by exaiming the case of one commodity per period. Individual choices will be the solutions to the following problem of constrained maximization,

$$\text{Max } u^t(c^t(t), c^t(t+1)), \qquad \text{subject to}$$

(III.1) $$p(t)c^t(t)+p(t+1)c^t(t+1) \leq p(t)w^t(t)+p(t+1)w^t(t+1),$$

where the right hand side is the value (at the ruling prices) of the resources of agent t. This maximization problem is depicted in Figure III.1.

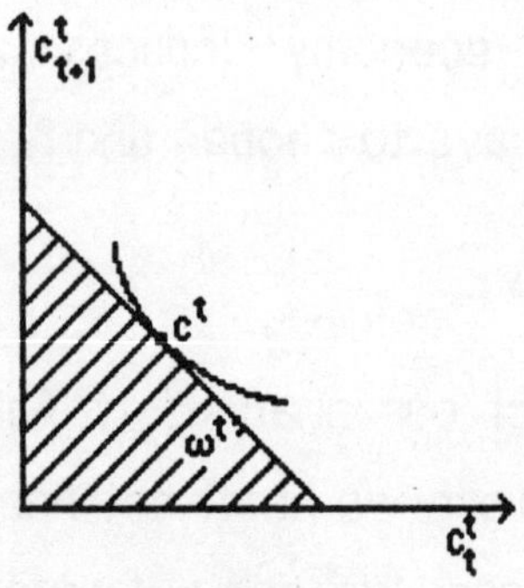

Figure III.1

The solution to this problem will satisfy the following first order conditions

(III.2) $$MRS^t(c^t)=p(t)/p(t+1)\equiv\pi^t \quad , \text{ and}$$

(III.3) $$p(t)c^t(t)+ p(t+1)c^t (t+1)=p(t)w^t(t)+p(t+1)w^t(t+1)\equiv R^t,$$

where π^t stands for the relative prices faced by generation t and R^t for the value of available lifetime resources. Condition (III.3) can be rewritten as

(III.4) $$\pi^t z^t(\pi^t,w^t)+x^t(\pi^t,w^t)=0,$$

where z^t is the excess demand in the first period, that is $z^t(t)= c^t(t) - w^t(t)$, and x^t is excess demand in the second period, $x^t=c^t(t+1) - w^t(t+1)$. We shall assume that both goods, $c^t(t)$ and $c^t(t+1)$, are non-inferior goods, that is, $\partial c^t(t)/\partial R^t>0$ and $\partial c^t(t+1)/\partial R^t>0$.

Consumption demand $c^t(t+s)$ will be a funtion of relative prices and endowments. Let us denote by $\bar{\pi}$ the prices at which agents do not wish to trade, that is, $z^t(\bar{\pi}^t)=x^t(\bar{\pi}^t)=0$. Indeed such prices always exist and correspond to the supporting prices at the endowment point.

Let us now define the indirect utility funtion v^t as

$$v^t(\pi^t,w^t)=u^t(w^t(t)+z^t(\pi^t),w^t(t+1)+x^t(\pi^t)).$$

We can now prove the following Proposition.

Proposition III.1 The following inequalities hold for any relative prices π :

a) $v^t(\pi^t, w^t) \geqq v^t(\bar{\pi}^t, w^t)$;

(III.5) b) $(\bar{\pi}^t - \pi^t)\, z^t(\pi^t) \geqq 0$, with strict inequalities for $\pi \neq \bar{\pi}$;

(III.6) c) $z^t(\pi^t) > 0$ as $\pi^t < \bar{\pi}^t$ and $z^t(\pi^t) < 0$ as $\pi^t > \bar{\pi}^t$; and

d) $\partial z^t / \partial p(t) < 0$ for $\pi^t \leqq \bar{\pi}^t$, and $\partial x^t / \partial p(t) > 0$ for $\pi^t \geqq \bar{\pi}^t$.

Proof.- Part a) follows from the fact that consumers can always choose $c^t = w^t$. Therefore the utility they reach when making different choices must be higher. Part b) follows from a revealed preference argument. Because of a), it must be that at prices $\bar{\pi}^t$ the choice $(w^t(t) + z^t(\pi^t), w^t(t+1) + x^t(\pi^t))$ violates the budget constraint, that is $\bar{\pi}^t z^t(\pi^t, w^t) + x^t(\pi^t, w^t) \geqq 0$. Using now (III.3) we obtain b). Part c) is a direct implication of b).

We can decompose $\partial z^t / \partial p(t)$ as

$$\partial z^t / \partial p(t) = \partial c^t(t) / \partial p(t) = \partial c^t(t) / \partial p(t)\big|_{R^t = ct.} + \\ + \partial c^t(t) / \partial R^t \cdot \partial R^t / \partial p(t).$$

The first term can in turn be decomposed into the substitution and income effects, so that

$$\partial c^t(t) / \partial p(t) = \partial^2 g^t / \partial p(t)^2 - c^t(t) \cdot \partial c^t(t) / \partial R^t + w^t(t) \cdot \partial c^t(t) / \partial R^t,$$

where g^t is the minimum expenditure function and therefore $\partial g^t/\partial p(t)$ is the compensated demand function and $\partial^2 g^t/\partial p(t)^2$ is the substitution effect, which is strictly negative. Rearranging terms we have that

$$\partial z^t/\partial p(t) = \partial c^t(t)/\partial p(t) = \partial^2 g^t/\partial p(t)^2 - z^t \cdot \partial c^t(t)/\partial R^t.$$

For $\pi^t \leqq \bar{\pi}^t$ we have that $z^t \geqq 0$ and therefore the natural assumption that first period consumption is a non-inferior good is sufficient to ensure that $\partial z^t/\partial p(t) < 0$.

As for $\partial x^t/\partial p(t)$ we can follow the same steps and write

$$\partial x^t/\partial p(t) = \partial c^t(t+1)/\partial p(t) = \partial^2 g^t/\partial p(t+1)\partial p(t) - z^t \cdot \partial c^t(t+1)/\partial R^t.$$

The first term is the cross substitution effect, which is positive. With the assumption that consumption at the old age is not an inferior good, the sign of the second term depends on the sign of the excess demand. In that case, for $\pi^t \geqq \bar{\pi}^t$ the excess demand z^t is non-positive and therefore we have that $\partial x^t/\partial p(t) > 0$ for $\pi^t \geqq \bar{\pi}^t$.QED.

We have singled out the relative prices $\bar{\pi}$, which induce agents to observe an autarkic behaviour. They will play a significant role later in this Chapter. Proposition III.1.a tells us that from the viewpoint of consumers $t=1,2,\ldots$, $\bar{\pi}$ is the worse possible price sequence.

With one commodity per period, excess demands and supplies can be easily interpreted as saving or dissaving. Specifically, $-p^t z^t(\pi^t)$ is the value of savings of consumer t when young. Then, Proposition II.6.c shows that individuals will save if and only if $\pi^t \geqq \bar{\pi}^t$.

This result is in fact stronger than in looks at first sight. From standard consumer theory we have developed the intuition that, except for pathological preferences (Giffen goods), the demand for a good varies inversely with its own price. The substitution effect reinforces the income effect. In our case, and in general when individual income depends on the market value of his endowments, the effects of a variation in prices are richer and the sign of the total effect harder to establish. Indeed, besides the standard income and substitution effects (for constant nominal income), here a price increase raises the nominal value of individual resources R^t. However, for $\pi^t > \bar{\pi}^t$ the two terms will have opposite signs and no general statement on the sign of the derivative will be possible. Note though that the sign is strict at $\bar{\pi}^t$ and that, by the continuity of the excess demand function, the sign should thus be preserved in the neighbourhood of $\bar{\pi}^t$. Unfortunately, throughout this chapter we shall mostly deal with equilibria with $\pi^t > \bar{\pi}^t$ and at some point we shall need to introduce the assumption that preferences are such that $\partial z^t/\partial p(t) < 0$ for all π.

Finally, it should be noted that the present observation shows that the popular belief that higher interest rates always increase savings is not well founded.

III.2. Competitive Equilibrium

We shall now examine the consumption allocations that can be a feasible outcome when agents behave competitively. In the previous section we have studied the choice of commodity net demands as a response to observed prices when agents behave competitively. However, those choices will in general not materialize in net demands that are feasible for the aggregate of the economy. As it is standard in equilibrium analysis we shall call "competitive equilibrium" to those special outcomes that have the property of being feasible for the economy. Similarly we shall call "equilibrium prices" to those prices that induce equilibrium outcomes.

At any period t aggregate excess demand will be the addition of the excess demands of the young generation just born in t and of the old generation born in the previous period $t-1$. Therefore, prices π^{t-1} and π^t will generate a market equilibrium at period t if

(III.7) $$z^t(\pi^t) + x^{t-1}(\pi^{t-1}) = 0.$$

Since the budget constraint (III.4) has to hold as an equality for any price sequence, we can rewrite the equilibrium condition (III.7) as

(III.8) $$z^t(\pi^t) - \pi^{t-1} z^{t-1}(\pi^{t-1}) = 0.$$

We can now introduce an interesting property of equilibrium price sequences. This property establishes that equilibrium price sequences can never "cross" the autarkic price sequence $\bar{\pi} = \{\bar{\pi}^1, \bar{\pi}^2, \ldots\}$.

Proposition III.2 Let π be a price sequence satistying (III.8) for t=2,3,... . Then, either $\pi^t = \bar{\pi}^t$, t=2,3,...; $\pi^t > \bar{\pi}^t$, t=2,3,... ; or $\pi^t < \bar{\pi}^t$, t=2,3,... .

<u>Proof</u>.- Observe first that if $\pi^{t-1} = \bar{\pi}^{t-1}$, condition (III.8) requires that $z^t(\pi^t) = 0$, that is, that $\pi^t = \bar{\pi}^t$. This proves the first part of the assertion. The second and third part easily follows from applying Proposition III.1 b) and c). QED.

In standard general equilibrium analysis Walras' Law plays an important role. It tells us that if n-1 markets are in equilibrium, then we need not to check whether the last market is in equilibrium. In other words, one of the n equilibrium conditions is redundant. The Walras Law is obtained by adding up all individual budget equalities and tells us that the aggregate value of excess demands is zero. It should be immediate that Walras Law cannot be directly applied to Overlapping Generations models. However, we can explore the implications of adding up the budget equalities of the infinite sequence of consumers. As we shall now see, this procedure will provide us with an important result on the behaviour of the value of net savings along the equilibrium paths.

Proposition III.3 Let π be a price sequence satistying (III.8) for t=2,3,... . Then

(III.9) $$p(t)\, z^t(\pi^t) = p(t-1)\, z^{t-1}(\pi^{t-1}) = z^1(\pi^1).$$

<u>Proof</u>.- The result (III.9) immediately follows from equilibrium condition (III.8) and from the fact that $\pi^{t-1} = p(t-1)/p(t)$. QED.

It should be noted that this result is stronger than Proposition III.2 because it shows that not only the sign of excess demands but the value too remains unchanged along an equilibrium path.

Equilibrium condition (III.8) gives us a difference equation. In order to determine the full equilibrium sequence of commodity prices we need only to fix the initial conditions. Therefore, let us turn to the markets clearing condition for period 1. In that initial period the plans of agents t=0 and t=1 need to be matched. In the previous section we have studied the behaviour of consumers along the two periods they are alive and this obviously describes the behaviour of generation t=1. However, generation t=0 is a different case all together. Their preferences are defined over the commodities that are available during this last period of their lifetime. The maximization program for generation t=0 is

$$\max u^0(c^0(1)) \text{ , subject to } p(1)c^0(1) \leqq p(1)w^0(1).$$

For the case of one commodity per period, the solution to this maximization program is trivial. The optimal choice consists in fully exhausting the available resources.Therefore $x^0(p(1)) = 0$ for all p(1), and specifically $x^0(1)=0$.

We can now turn to the equilibrium condition for period $t=1$, which is $z^1(\pi^1) + x^0(1) = 0$.

Therefore, we have that the equilibrium value of π^1 has to satisfy that $z^1(\pi^1)=0$ and thus $\pi^1 = \bar{\pi}^1$. By Propositions III.2 and III.3 we have that $\pi^t = \bar{\pi}^t$, $t=1,2,\ldots$, and that the equlibrium value of net savings is zero along the entire path. Further, this equilibrium is unique.

We have thus proven the following Proposition.

Proposition III.4 Let there be one good per period and one agent per generation. Then a competitive equilibrium exists and has the following properties:

i) it is unique;

ii) $\pi^t = \bar{\pi}^t$, $t=1,2,\ldots$, and

iii) $p(t)z^t(\pi^t) = 0$, $t=1,2,\ldots$.

Proof.- Follows from the previous discussion. QED.

From a general equilibrium point of view this result is important because it shows us of a case in which, in spite of the fact that a full set of markets is available, future markets turn out not to operate. We have thus an example of a model in which the inexistence of some markets is an endogenous result and not a starting assumption. The reason for this result is that real world agents are imperfectly coordinated because of the fact of life that agents live for a finite length of time and that at any point new consumers come in, while others disappear.

In our simple model, for prices at which agents want to save when young, consumers cannot find another agent interested in matching the complementary trade. That is why no equilibrium path can sustain a positive amount of aggregate savings. In the next Chapter we shall see how the introduction of paper, fiat money can vastly increase the set of feasible trades.

The last section of this Chapter is devoted to the extensions of the results presented here to the case of many commodities per period. However, we wish to point out that the result about the uniqueness of competitive equilibria depends crucially, not only on the hypothesis of one good per period, but also on the assumption that consumers live for two periods only.

Before going into other properties of competitive equilibria let us briefly discuss the problem of the "number" of equilibria when consumers live for more than two periods. We shall simply assume that the lifespan of individuals extends over 3 periods: youth, middle age, and old days. The maximization program of a typical consumer will be

$$\max u(c^t(t), c^t(t+1), c^t(t+2))$$

$$\text{subject to } \pi^t \pi^{t+1} z^t + \pi^{t+1} x^t + y^t \leqq 0,$$

where y denotes the excess demand on the third period of life. Of course, the optimal solution will generate excess demands that depend on π^t and π^{t+1}, and the budget constraint will be satisfied as an equality, i.e.depend on

$$\pi^t \pi^{t+1} z^t + \pi^{t+1} x^t + y^t = 0.$$

Equilibrium at period t will now be

$$z^t(\pi^t, \pi^{t+1}) + x^{t-1}(\pi^{t-1}, \pi^t) + y^{t-2}(\pi^{t-2}, \pi^{t-1}) = 0 \ , \ t=2,3,...,$$

and

$$z^1(\pi^1, \pi^2) + x^0(\pi^1) + y^{-1}(1) = 0, \text{ for } t=1.$$

The equilibrium condition for $t \geqq 2$ depends on four relative prices, but some may have been determined as equilibrium conditions for past periods. Let us therefore start at period $t=1$. We know that $y^{-1}(1)=0$, because those agents are not going to live in the next period. The middle aged agents will still have a genuine intertemporal problem distributing their resources between present and future, when they will be old. Therefore, market equilibrium at $t=1$ gives one equation but depends on two unknown relative prices : π^1 and π^2. If we now consider the simultaneous equilibrium at periods $t=1,2$, we add a new equilibrium equation but a new unknown price wit it, π^3. Therefore, we shall generally have a continuum of equilibria : the solution of the model is indeterminate (in a strong sense)[1].

Let us now finally examine the efficiency of competitive equilibria in Overlapping Generations models. In finite Arrow-Debreu economies we have the well known Fundamental Welfare Theorems establishing that competitive equilibria are Pareto efficient and that all Pareto optimal allocations can be obtained as a competitive equilibrium after a suitable redistribution of individual resources. The First Fundamental Theorem, though, does not hold true for Overlapping Generations economies.

Proposition III.5 In Overlapping Generations economies competitive equilibria may not be Pareto optimal.

Proof.- From Proposition III.4 it is clear that the competitive consumption allocation sequence consists in equating consumption to endowments period by period for every agent and that the equilibrium prices are $\bar{\pi}^t = MRS^t(w^t)$. From Proposition II.5 we know that this consumption allocation is Pareto optimal if and only if $\Sigma 1/\bar{p}^t = +\infty$. Further, from Proposition II.2 we know that we can construct economies such that Pareto inefficient allocations do exist. QED.

We thus have that Overlapping Generations economies are an example of a plausible description of an economy in which the choices of competitive agents coordinated through markets do not lead to efficient outcomes. A possible interpretation of this result is that in as much as this model captures essential elements of the world, the typical state of affairs would then be an active intervention of the government in order to achieve optimality. One can object to this interpretation that in this model agents turn out to behave as if the available markets structure were incomplete, with the futures markets not being operative. From this observation one could infer that Proposition III.5 is just an implication of the fact that only spot markets are really open for transactions.

The possible Pareto inefficiency of competitive equilibria when the market structure is incomplete has been established long ago[2]. It is precisely in this area that the alternative notion of "restricted optimality" has been put forward as a substitute for Pareto efficiency. The argument would be as follows. The assumption that some markets do not operate simply reflects the existence of some constraints that are outside the scope of the model. When we inquire about the efficiency of a given consumption allocation we place our selves in the position of a planner with full control over the existing resources. We then investigate whether the allocation consumption goods could have been improved in the Pareto sense. It is then argued that the same unexamined restrictions that account for the incompleteness of markets should restrict the planner when considering alternative distributions. The implication of this argument is then that under these circumstances it is not sensible the concept of "unrestricted" optimality. One should instead use the notion of "restricted" efficiency, taking into account the existing social constraints.

Following these steps, the notion of "restricted" efficiency in Overlapping Generations economies should take into account that futures markets do not operate and, therefore, that no reallocation involving intertemporal transfers should be considered actually feasible. It is then immediate that "restricted" efficiency is identical to weak Pareto optimality.

We can now demonstrate that competitive equilibria are always weakly efficient.

Proposition III.6 Let the consumption allocation sequence c be a competitive equilibrium. Then it is weakly Pareto optimal.

<u>Proof</u>.- From Proposition II.1 we know that a necessary and sufficient condition for weak efficiency is that

$$c^t(t) + c^{t-1}(t) = w^t(t)+w^{t-1}(t), \qquad t=1,2,\dots .$$

If c is not weakly Pareto optimal there must exist some t_0 such that

$$c^{t_0}(t_0) + c^{t_0-1}(t_0) < w^{t_0}(t_0)+w^{t_0-1}(t_0).$$

But this would contradict the assumption that c is a competitive equilibrium. QED.

We shall now show the converse result. We shall demonstrate that every weakly Pareto optimal consumption allocation can be implemented as a competitive equilibrium after a suitable redistribution of initial endowments.

Proposition III.7 Let the consumption allocation sequence c be weakly Pareto optimal. Then there exist a sequence of initial endowments w and a sequence of prices p for which c is a competitive equilibrium.

Proof.- From Proposition II.1 we know that a necessary and sufficient condition for weakly efficiency is that

$$c^t(t) + c^{t-1}(t) = \overline{w}(t)\ ,\ t=1,2, \dots .$$

Therefore, let us consider the initial endowments sequence $w^t = c^t$, $t=0,1,2,\dots$ and the price sequence p such that $p(t)/p(t+1) = MRS^t(c^t)$. Since individual utility functions are strictly increasing and strictly quasi-concave, for every $\tilde{c}^t \neq c^t$ such that $u^t(\tilde{c}^t) \geqq u^t(c^t)$ it must be that

$$p(t)\tilde{c}^t(t)+p(t+1)\tilde{c}^t(t+1)>p(t)c^t(t)+p(t+1)c^t(t+1).$$

Since $w^t=c^t$, it follows that c^t maximizes individual utility over the set of all x^t such that $p(t)\tilde{c}^t(t)+p(t+1)\tilde{c}^t(t+1) \leqq p(t)w^t(t)+p(t+1)w^t(t+1)$. Therefore, c is a competitive equilibrium. QED.

Propositions III.6 and III.7 are versions of the First and Second Fundamental Theorems of Welfare Economics, respectively, for Overlapping Generations Economies. Therefore the concept of weak Pareto optimality in Overlapping Generations models seems to play the same role as Pareto optimality in Arrow-Debreu economies. However, the argument for weak Pareto optimality is not free from objections.

The overlapping structure of the population of consumers, responsible for the non operation of the futures markets, does not actually constrain the choices available to a planner. As we shall see in the next section, the introduction of a simple device (paper money) can produce Pareto efficient (monetary) competitive equilibria.

Moreover, the previous result is quite specific to the one good model. With many goods per period agents do trade in equilibrium, but on spot markets only. With many (and different) agents futures markets operate but the agents trading in those markets belong to the same generation. In that case, therefore, the restriction imposed by the overlapping structure of the population of consumers is that net aggregate savings of each generation are nil in equilibrium. Finally, when agents live for many periods, the restriction becomes that the net aggregate savings for all the living generations but the oldest have to be zero in equilibrium. Therefore, under a sufficiently general perspective, the argument for "restricted" optimality seems to be ill based.

III.3. Competitive Equilibria with many Commodities

In this section we shall briefly present the extension of the model to the n-commodity case.

We shall denote by $c^t(i,t+s)$ the consumption of commodity i at period $t+s$ by agent t, $i= 1,\dots,n$, $s=0,1$, by $c^t \in \mathbb{R}^{2n}_+$ the consumption of agent t in the two periods he is alive, i.e.

$c^t=(c^t(t),c^t(t+1))$. Since generation 0 will be alive for the period $t=1$ only, his consumption will simply be $c^0=c^0(1)$. A consumption allocation is a sequence c specifying the consumption assigned to each consumer in every period t, i.e. $c = \{c^0, c^1, c^2, \dots\}$.

We shall denote by $w^t(i,t+s)$ the initial endowment of agent t of the good i available at period $t+s, i=1,\dots,n, s=0,1$, and $w^t \in \mathbb{R}^{2n}_+$ the vector of endowments corresponding to the two periods that the agent will be alive. Again, for generation $t=0$ we have that $w^0=w^0(1)$. Aggregate endowments at period t will be denoted by $w(t)$, i.e. $w(t)=w^{t-1}(t)+w^t(t)$, $w(t)\in\mathbb{R}^n_+$. Finally, we shall let w be the sequence $w=\{w^0, w^1, w^2,\dots\}$.

Preferences of consumer t can be represented by a utility function $u^t:\mathbb{R}^{2n}_+ \to \mathbb{R}$, for $t=1,2,\dots$ and $u^0:\mathbb{R}^n_+ \to \mathbb{R}$, for $t=0$. We shall assume that u^t is differentiable strictly increasing and strictly quasi-concave.

We shall still restrict to rational expectation, self-fulfilling equilibria. We shall denote by $p(i,t)$ the price of commodity i delivered at period t, by $p(t)$ the n-dimensional vector of prices at t and by p the price sequence $p=\{p(1), p(2),\dots\}$.

Individual choices will be the solutions to the following problem of constrained maximization,

$$\text{Max } u^t(c^t(t),c^t(t+1)), \qquad \text{subject to}$$

$$\text{(III.10)} \quad p(t)\cdot c^t(t)+p(t+1)\cdot c^t(t+1) \leqq p(t)\cdot w^t(t)+p(t+1)\cdot w^t(t+1), \quad t=1,2,\ldots$$

$$\text{and} \qquad \text{Max } u^0(c^0(1)), \qquad \text{subject to}$$

$$p(1)\cdot c^0(1) \leqq p(1)\cdot w^0(1).$$

where the right hand side is the value of the resources of agent t.

We shall denote by z^t and x^t the excess demands for the first and second period. Therefore, $z^t: \mathbb{R}^{2n}{}_+ \to \mathbb{R}^n{}_+$ and $x^t: \mathbb{R}^{2n}{}_+ \to \mathbb{R}^n{}_+$ and $x^0: \mathbb{R}^n{}_+ \to \mathbb{R}^n{}_+$. Further, we shall have that

$$\text{(III.11)} \qquad p(t)\cdot z^t(p(t),p(t+1))+p(t+1)\cdot x^t(p(t),p(t+1)) = 0, \quad t=1,2,\ldots \text{ and}$$

$$p(1)\cdot x^0(p(1)) = 0.$$

A price sequence p is a competitive equilibrium if markets clear at every period, that is

$$\text{(III.12)} \qquad z^t(p(t),p(t+1)) + x^{t-1}(p(t-1),p(t)) = 0, \quad t = 1,2,\ldots .$$

In order to examine the existence and uniqueness of competitive equilibria we shall closely follow Balasko and Shell [4][3]. For this purpose they study first the behaviour of finite T-economies, as defined in Section II.2. A T-equilibrium price sequence p for a T-economy will be a price sequence that generates a feasible consumption allocation for the T-economy, as in (II.1). Since a T-economy is a pure exchange Arrow-Debreu economy satisfying the desirable properties, it is clear that there will exist T-equilibrium price sequences for any finite T.

Due to the fact that we do not require markets to clear in T+1, we have an additional degree of freedom so that we shall typically have many T-equilibrium price sequences. Let P(T) be the set of such sequences. It is then easy to see that $P(T+1) \subseteq P(T)$. We can now state the existence result.

Proposition III.8 [Balasko and Shell [4]] In an Overlapping Generations economy there always exists a competitive equilibrium price sequence associated with every sequence of endowments.

Proof.- We have just pointed out that the T-equilibrium price sets are nested. Moreover, it is not difficult to prove that these T-equilibrium price sets are compact.

The competitive equilibrium price sequence for the full infinite economy belongs to the intersection of the sequence of sets P(T). But the intersection of a sequence of nested non-empty and compact sets is non-empty. QED.

We have seen in the previous section that it is specific of the one-good , two-period lifetime model that competitive equilibria are unique. Indeed we have shown there that the mere extension to three-period lived agents leads to the existence of multiple equilibria, possibly a continuum. The same result obtains when we extend to model to an n-commodities economy, while keeping the two-period hypothesis. After all, as pointed out by Balasko, Cass and Shell [3], the distinction between the two cases is nominal only.

Market clearing conditions in any period t defines n equations

$$z^t(p(t),p(t+1)) + x^{t-1}(p(t-1),p(t)) = 0 \ , \ t = 1,2,\ldots \ .$$

But we have 3n variables, although provision has to be made by the degrees of freedom generated by the homogeneity of excess demand functions. In the first period p(0) will be known past information. But we shall still be left with 2n unknowns. Kehoe and Levine [] have studied the special case of stationary environments and shown that even when restricting to equilibrium sequences converging to stationary solutions equilibrium sequences may be an n-1 dimensional manifold. Santos [53] has proven that without the stationarity restriction and considering all the equilibrium price sequences one can have n-dimensional manifolds.

It is clear that strong indeterminacy will not be exceptional. We shall now study a special class of economies for which competitive equilibria are unique. As in Section II.3, we shall assume intertemporal separability of individual preferences. We pointed out there that this allows for decomposing the intertemporal allocation of resources into the intra-period and the interperiod allocation[4]. We can thus define the (t,t+1) economy by the second period preferences of agent t, $v^t_{t+1}(c^t(t+1))$, and the first period preferences of agent t+1,

$v^{t+1}{}_{t+1}(c^{t+1}(t+1))$, together with the corresponding endowments $w^t(t+1)$ and $w^{t+1}(t+1)$.

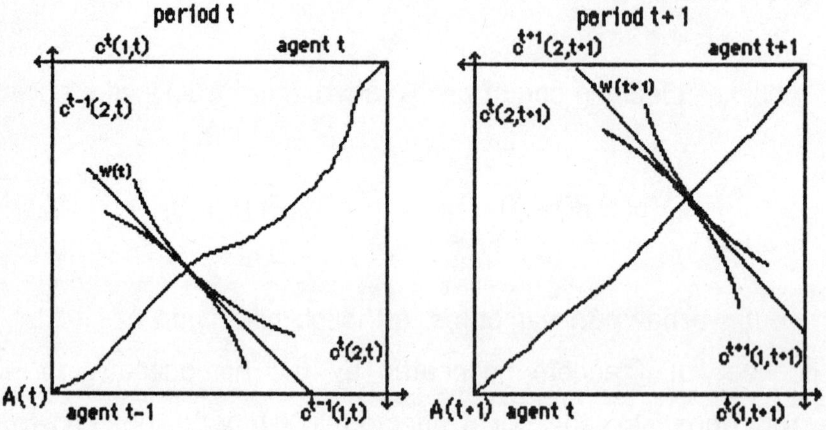

Figure III.2

Therefore, in order to obtain an equilibrium price sequence we first identify equilibrium n-dimensional price vectors $\bar{p}(t+1)$ for each (t,t+1) economy, as depicted in Figure III.2. Because of the homogeneity of excess demand funtions we can normalize these price vectors by chosing $\bar{p}(1,t) = 1$, $t=1,2,\ldots$. Then we can find the sequence $\pi(t)$, with $\pi(1) = 1$, such that for the price sequence p , $p(t) = \pi(t)\cdot\bar{p}(t)$, $t=1,2,\ldots$, for which the equilibrium consumption allocation is utility maximazing. Clearly the ratio between $\pi(t)$ and $\pi(t+1)$ stands for the intertemporal rate of substitution.

Under the present assumptions it is easy to prove that for a given sequence $\bar{p}$, the sequence π is uniquely determined. Therefore, the uniqueness of the equilibrium price sequence p entirely depends on the uniqueness of $\bar{p}(t)$. Specifically, the equilibrium sequence p is unique if and only if $\bar{p}(t)$ is unique for t=1,2,... .

It is well known that either gross substitutability or that aggregate demand functions satisfy the Weak Axiom of revealed preferences are sufficient conditions for the existence of unique a equilibrium in pure exchange economies. Therefore, that either of the two conditions be satisfied for every (t,t+1) economy is a sufficient condition for uniqueness of the competitive equilibrium[5]. If $\bar{p}(t)$ is not unique for a finite number of periods we shall have multiple but finite equilibria. But if $\bar{p}(t)$ is not unique for a subsequence of periods the economy will a countable infinity of equilibria, as shown by Geanakoplos and Polemarchakis [30] and Kehoe and Levine[40]. Multiplicity of equilibria is thus the rule and not the exception.

It is obvious that this vast multiplicity of equilibria is troublesome. It simply means that the model laid down to examine the intertemporal allocation of resources gives indeterminate answers. It is a matter for future research to find a natural way to eliminate all but a finite number of equilibria. The viability of intertemporal allocations examined in Part III of this book can be seen as a way of discarding unreachable equilibria. However, as we shall see later, the trustworthiness of the different equilibria is not a sufficient condition for the selection of a finite number of equilibria.

Notes to Chapter III

1 Kehoe and Levine [40] have thoroughly studied the degree of indeterminacy in Overlapping Generations models. The point that we may have indeterminacy in such a simple model as the one considered here with three periods of life was first made by these authors. See also Santos [52] and [53].

2 See Hart [35] and Grossman [33].

3 One can find an equilibrium existence theorem under more general assumptions in Balasko, Cass and Shell [3].

4 The multiplicity of equilibria with intertemporaly separable preferences has been studied by Geanakoplos and Polemarchakis [30] and Kehoe and Levine [40].

5 Balasko and Shell [6] show that for separable, log-linear utility functions the competitive equilibrium is unique.

Chapter IV Monetary Equilibria

IV.1 The role of money

Before extending our previous analysis of competitive equilibria to economies with money, let us discuss in some detail the role of money in general equilibrium models and the suitability of Overlapping Generations models for the foundations of Monetary Theory.

Monetary economies can only be meaningfully described when they are modelled in such a way that room is left for money to play a specific role. R. Clower [18] has expressed this need by stressing the fact that «commodities do not buy commodities». Commodities can be sold for money and with money we can then buy goods, that is, money serves as an intermediary in the transactions process. Not surprisingly, this problem has been traditionaly neglected in General Equilibrium Theory because of the all pervading role assigned to the auctioneer in organizing the exchange. In the standard description, agents do not visit specific markets and face other agents acting as sellers or buyers because all net demands are surrendered to the auctioneer and the meeting of needs is organized through him.

The first fundamental point to be made is that in a monetary economy we shall have to dispense with the auctioneer as the intermediator of all exchanges. Consequently, the problem of exchange will have to be modelled explicitly. This has been done in a variety of ways each giving rise to a family of models focussing on different aspects of the process of exchange.

The first attempt at expressing these views was that of Keynes. The notion of liquidity and the idea that effective demand may be constrained by the lack of liquidity, implicitly assumes that exchanges have to be made with the intermediation of money. The modelling of the idea however did not go very far. He assumed the existence of a demand function for money as a means of exchange, which essentially depends on the volume of transactions, i.e. on output, and possibly the interest rate. Since in his model the real commodities are "output" and "labour", one has to presume that what he had in the back of his mind was that labour cannot purchase commodities directly, but needs the intermediation of money. This transactions demand for money is then added to the "speculative" demand for money (resulting from the role of money as a store of value) to form the aggregate demand for money. The comfrontation of this aggregate demand for money with the government controlled supply of money gives rise to the equilibrium condition known as the "LM curve". This line of thought has been pursued by the many neo-keynesian theories of the transactions demand for money[1].

Patinkin [49] was possibly the first attempt at integrating Monetary Theory with General Equilibrium Theory by means of introducing the money balances into the utility functions of economic agents. Money is desired and thus can obtain a positive market price. This is a clever device to provide a common framework for the study of money within the general problem of resource allocation. However it has the drawback that does not throw any light on why money is valuable for consumers. Most of the contemporary Monetary Theory tries to provide an answer to this question.

The essential contribution of Clower [18] consists in addressing explicitly the problem of exchange. He starts by positing the principle that commodities do not buy commodities, but money which acts as an intermediary. He then goes into expressing these restrictions by means of a transactions technology matrix. The elements of this matrix are either zeroes or ones and simply tell us whether direct transactions between goods k and j are possible for agent i. Individual choice is thus constrained not only by the budget set as defined by the endowments and the ruling prices, but by these exchange constraints as well. In this way consumers will have to demand money as a counterpart of their sale of some goods. The main virtue of Clower's contribution is that he pointed towards the fundamental idea in modeling monetary economies: agents do not face a single, standard budget constraint, but a series of constraints reflecting the restrictions in the trading process.

Let us now take back the original idea that we need to specify how exchange takes place in the absence of the auctioneer. After all, Clower's idea of a transactions technology is but one amongst the many possible specifications of the restrictions that appear when we leave to individuals the organization of exchange. Restrictions in the possible exchanges can be specified at different levels of intensity.

Let us start by the simplest case: the structure of markets is incomplete, but there is no coordination problem. In order to have an appropriate point of reference let us consider the Arrow-Debreu model with many periods or different states of the world and uncertainty. One can model this generalization by enlarging the commodity space and the number of markets. Each dated commodity is traded in a different market ("spot" and "futures" markets) and each commodity in each state of the world is again a distinct good and traded in a specific market, i.e. the "contingent" markets. This way of conceiving the proble tends to eliminate the effect of time or uncertainty. All transactions can take place at present by means of suitable transactions in the futures or in the contingent markets. However, we do not observe such a rich structure of markets[2]. It seems thus useful to examine the working of the economy with an incomplete structure of markets. As a matter of fact, the assumption implicit in the Overlapping Generations model that there is no pair of generations of agents that fully overlap in all the markets they are interested in is just a way of motivating the incompleteness of the market structure.

The very nature of markets in the Arrow-Debreu model is quite obscure. An exchange is a two sided operation by which some quantities fo different goods change hands. The question emerges as to what is the counterpart of an exchange in the Arrow-Debreu model. Suppose that we receive bread in exchange for labour. The problem is then that since bread would be traded in a variety of markets, we could not properly speak of "the bread market". We thus have two options: either implicit in the model agents exchange goods for money or the very idea of one market for each good should be simply abandoned. The first alternative seems the most sensible, but hard to accomodate within the Arrow-Debreu model. Where does the money come from?, how is it soaked from the system? how is it that money does not show up in the constraints restricting individual choice?. Observe that talking of "buying" and "selling" presupposes the exchange of goods for money. In a barter trade there is neither a buyer nor a seller, there is mutual exchange of commodities. The second alternative point to modeling the economy as composed of $(n-1)^2$ markets, a typical market consisting in the exchange of spot diamonds for pencils, for instance. But in that case some exchanges might not be possible. In an example due to Cass and Yaari [9] with four agents, agent 1 demands good 1 and supplies 2, agent 2 demands 2 and supplies 3, agent 3 demands 3 and supplies 4 and finally agent 4 demands 4 and supplies 1. Even if all 3^2 markets were operative, there would be no transactions because in this example there would be no mutal coincidence of wants. But even if this problem would not exist, still the introduction of money could be quite beneficial. It would drastically simply the necessary information and it would cut down the number of markets to its square root (plus one) thus increasing competition in each of the surviving "monetarized" markets. This is the standard problem contamplated in the general equilibrium models focussing on the transactions costs.

In the light of the foregoing discussion, the Overlapping Generation model can be interpreted as a model that provides a demographic explanation for the lack of full coincidence of wants. Young and old cannot undergo in any intertemporal exhange. This impossibility of intertemporal trades through markets could have been reworded as a case with infinite costs of transaction between present and future. The role of money in the Overlapping Generations model is thus not essentially different from other (static) general equilibrium models with transactions costs in which Monetary Theory was framed during the 70's. In both cases money eliminates transactions costs and allows the economy to reach competitive equilibria that would have been unattainable otherwise.

IV.2. Consumer Behaviour in a Monetary Economy

In the previous Chapters we have described an economy in which, in spite of the availability of a complete set of markets, consumers end up using in equilibrium spot markets only. Our model then predicts that in this economy we would not observe the existence of future markets.

Our description of consumer behaviour in Section III.2. we have implicitly assumed that agents made their choice under the belief that all markets were operative. Let us now briefly reformulate the problem of consumer behaviour when his choice is subject to the additional restriction of the unexistence of some markets. This exercise will be a natural introduction to the analysis of consumer demand in a monetary economy.

The lack of futures markets has radical implication in our one-good model. Besides the standard budget constraint, consumers will now maximise under the additional restriction that they cannot transfer purchasing power from one period to the other. The program of constrained maximization now becomes,

$$\text{Max } u^t(c^t(t), c^t(t+1)), \qquad \text{subject to}$$

$$(\text{IV.1}) \qquad p(t)c^t(t) \leq p(t)w^t(t), \text{ and}$$

$$p(t+1)c^t(t+1) \leq p(t+1)w^t(t+1).$$

This maximization problem is depicted in Figure IV.1, where the shaded area is the attainable set for consumer t under the two constraints.

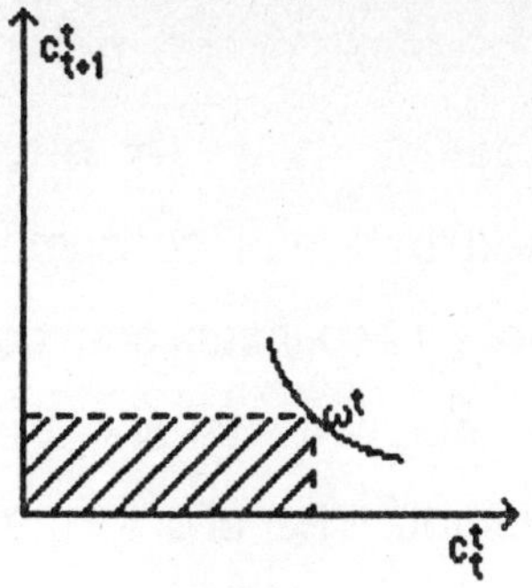

Figure IV.1

The solution to this maximization problem is, of course, trivial. The problem, however, becomes more interesting with many commodities.

Let us now examine how individual behaviour is altered by the introduction of money. Specifically, we shall assume that there is a new commodity called "money" that is intrinsically worthless, but that can be purchased and sold at a non-negative price q(t). This commodity has no direct effect on individual utility, but can be stored from one period to the next. It is a remarkable characteristic of Overlapping Generations models that makes such an inocuous object induce agents to attain equilibrium allocations that were unreachable without it and that rational agents are prepared to pay a strictly positive price for these printed pieces of paper. Money, of course, is a commodity that can only be held in non-negative amounts.

Futures markets do not operate, but now there is a new market: the market for money. Agents can buy some units of this commodity when they are young and sell it for consumption goods when they are old. We shall use m^t to denote the amount of money purchased by agent t, $m^t \geqq 0$. The decision problem is now split into two. When young agents have to decide how to allocate the value of their endowments in that period between consumption goods and money. In the second period available resources are composed of (the value of) the second period initial endowments and the money balances carried over from the previous period. Therefore, the maximization problem is

$$\text{Max } u^t(c^t(t), c^t(t+1)), \qquad \text{subject to}$$

$$\text{(IV.2)} \qquad p(t)c^t(t) + q(t)m^t \leqq p(t)w^t(t), \text{ and}$$

$$p(t+1)c^t(t+1) \leqq p(t+1)w^t(t+1) + q(t+1)m^t, \quad \text{with } m^t \geqq 0.$$

The standard budget constraint presented in Section IV.2 on consumer behaviour is here split into a sequence of two budget constraints. This constrained maximization problem is depicted in Figure IV.2.

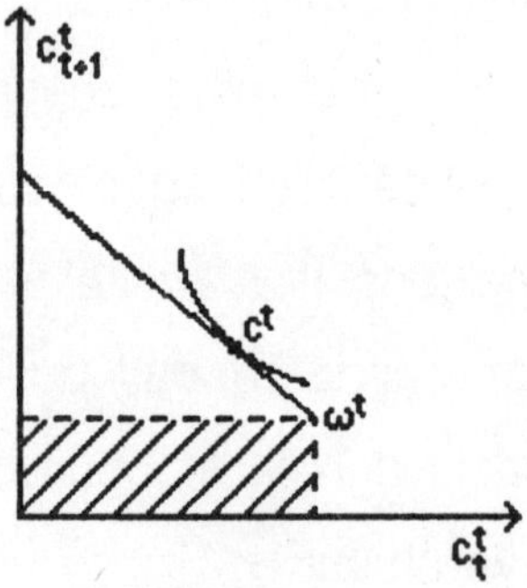

Figure IV.2

The solution of this problem will give us the demand for goods on the two spot markets and the demand for money when young.

We shall then have by Proposition III.1 that

(IV.3) $z^t=z^t(\pi^t)$ and $x^t=x^t(\pi^t)$ for $\pi^t \geqq \bar{\pi}^t$, $z^t=x^t=0$ for $\pi^t \leqq \bar{\pi}^t$,

and $m^t = -p(t)z^t/q(t)$ $t=1,2,\ldots$.

The first generation of old agents will now have money balances $\bar{m}$ and initial endowments of the consumption good[3]. Utility maximization leads this agent to an excess demand x^0 such that

(IV.4) $$x^0(1,q(1)\,\bar{m}) = q(1)\,\bar{m}.$$

IV.3. Monetary Equilibria

With the new excess demand functions we can now investigate the existence of monetary equilibria. A monetary equilibrium is a feasible competitive[4] consumption allocation generated by the price sequences p (or π) and q, with $q(t)>0$, $t=1,2,\ldots$. We shall follow the convention of calling "walrasian" those competitive equilibria that are attainable without the use of fiat money, or with $\bar{m}>0$ but $q(t)=0$ $t=1,2,\ldots$. Therefore, in this simple model competitive equilibria will be either walrasian or monetary, but in both cases we shall have market clearing, that is,

$$z^{t+1}(\pi^{t+1})+x^t(\pi^t)=0 \quad \text{for} \quad t=1,2,\ldots, \quad \text{and} \quad z^1(\pi^1)+x^0=0.$$

Differentiating the equilibrium condition we obtain

$$d\pi^{t+1}/d\pi^t = -(\partial x^t/\partial\pi^t)/(\partial z^{t+1}/\partial\pi^{t+1}).$$

From Proposition III.1.d we know that $\partial x^t/\partial\pi^t > 0$ for $\pi^t > \bar{\pi}^t$. We thus need now the assumption that $\partial z^t/\partial\pi^t < 0$ to establish that for every π^t there is a unique market clearing π^{t+1} and moreover that $d\pi^{t+1}/d\pi^t > 0$.

Before showing the existence of monetary equilibria it is useful examining some useful properties of these allocations.

Proposition IV.1 Let the consumption allocation c and the price sequences p and q be a monetary equilibrium. Then $q(t)=q$, $t=1,2,\dots$.

Proof.- From Proposition III.3 we know that for $\pi^t > \bar{\pi}^t$,

$$p(t)\, z^t(\pi^t) = p(t-1)\, z^{t-1}(\pi^{t-1}) = z^1(\pi^1).$$

From utility maximization we have that

$$q(t)m^t = -p(t)z^t(\pi^t) \qquad t=2,3,\dots, \text{ and}$$

$$x^0(1,q(1)\,\bar{m}) = q(1)\,\bar{m}.$$

Hence

$$q(t)m^t = -p(t)z^t(\pi^t) = -z^1(\pi^1).$$

Taking into account that money supply is constant and equal to $\overline{m}$, equilibrium in the money market requires that $m^t = \overline{m}$, $t=1,2,\ldots$. Therefore, in a monetary equilibrium $q(t)=q(1)=q$, $t=1,2,3,\ldots$. QED.

This property greatly simplifies our study of monetary equilibria. Besides the sequence of commodity prices, we need only looking for one single price for money. In spite of the fact that in real life we normalise prices by setting q=1, we shall use p(1)=1. After all, that q>0 is what has to be proven. Let us now prove existence of monetary equilibria.

The first relevant observation is that, while there always exists an equilibrium at prices $q=0$ and $\pi = \overline{\pi}$, a monetary equilibrium with q>0 may not exist. We shall now give a sufficient condition for the non existence of a monetary equilibrium.

Proposition IV.2 Let the walrasian equilibrium of the economy c be Pareto optimal. Then there is no monetary equilibrium with q>0. In other words, a necessary condition for the existence of a monetary equilibrium is that

$$\Sigma\, 1/\,\overline{p}(t) < +\infty.$$

Proof.- We shall prove this proposition by way of contradiction. Assume therefore that the walrasian allocation is Pareto optimal, but that there exists a monetary equilibrium allocation $\tilde{c}$ with commodity prices π and money price $q>0$. By

Proposition III.1.a we know that

$$v^t(\pi^t, w^t) \geqq v^t(\bar{\pi}^t, w^t), \text{ for } t=1,2,\ldots .$$

Further, $u^0(w^0(1)+q\,\bar{m}) > u^0(w^0(1))$, for $q>0$. Therefore $\tilde{c}$ Pareto dominates the walrasian equilibrium allocation c, and this contradicts the hypothesis that c was Pareto optimal. QED.

Let us now obtain a simple property of equilibrium price sequences for monetary equilibria that will be useful in the development of our analysis. It is another necessary condition for the existence of a monetary equilibrium.

Proposition IV.3 Let the consumption allocation sequence c with money supply $\bar{m}$ and prices π and $q>0$ be a monetary equilibrium. Then, a) $\operatorname{Lim\,inf}_{t\to\infty} p(t) > 0$, and b) $p(t) < \bar{p}(t)$, $t=2,3,\ldots$.

<u>Proof</u>.- In a monetary equilibrium market clearing requires that

$$-p(t)z^t(\pi^t) = q\,\bar{m}, \quad t=1,2,\ldots .$$

Further, from the boundedness of the endowments sequence we know that $z^t(\pi^t) \leqq w^t(t) < +\infty$. Therefore, if $\operatorname{Lim\,inf}_{t\to\infty} p(t) = 0$, the equilibrium condition will eventually be violated. This proves statement a).

We shall now prove part b). From Proposition III.1.c we

know that for monetary equilibria it must be true that $\pi^t > \bar{\pi}^t$, $t=1,2,\ldots$. Since $p(1)= \bar{p}(1)=1$, we have that $p(2)< \bar{p}(2)$ for $t=2$. For the next period we know that $\pi^2=p(2)/p(3)> \bar{p}(2)/\bar{p}(3)= \bar{\pi}^2$ and , therefore, $p(3)< \bar{p}(3)$. By repeating this argument we can obtain the desired result. Further, by use of Propositions III.1 and III.2 it can be readily proven that if a competitive equilibrium satisfies that $p(t)< \bar{p}(t)$, $t=2,3,\ldots$, it must be a monetary equilibrium. QED.

Before going into the most general case, let us start by examining the existence of monetary equilibria for stationary economies, i.e. economies in which every generation has the same preferences and the same endowments, $u^t(c^t)=u(c^t)$ and $w^t=(w^z,w^x)$ for $t=1,2,\ldots$. In such an economy excess demand functions are identical for all generations. The budget constraint then reads $\pi z(\pi)+x(\pi) = 0$ and the equilibrium condition as

$$(IV.5) \qquad z(\pi^{t+1})+x(\pi^t)=0 \quad \text{for } t=1,2,\ldots, \text{ and } z(\pi^1)=-x^0=q\,\bar{m}.$$

This equilibrium condition implicitly defines a difference equation in which π^{t+1} is a function of π^t . Differentiating we have that

$$d\pi^{t+1}/d\pi^t=- x'(\pi^t)/z'(\pi^{t+1}).$$

From the budget constraint we can obtain upon differentiation

$$x'(\pi^t)= - z(\pi^t) - \pi^t z'(\pi^t).$$

Substituting we can finally write,

(IV.6) $$d\pi^{t+1}/d\pi^{t} = [z(\pi^{t}) + \pi^{t} z'(\pi^{t})] / z'(\pi^{t+1}).$$

The relative prices corresponding to the walrasian equilibrium are $\bar{\pi}^t = \bar{\pi}$, t=1,2,... and therefore the equilibrium price sequence $\bar{p}$ satisfies $\bar{p}^{t+1} = (1/\bar{\pi})^t$, t=1,2, ... From this it follows that the walrasian equilibrium is Pareto optimal if and only if $\bar{\pi} \geqq 1$. We can now state the following existence result.

Proposition IV.4 Let a stationary Overlapping Generations economy have a walrasian equilibrium not Pareto optimal, i.e. $\bar{\pi}<1$. Then, if the excess demand z is a decreasing function, for a stock of money $\bar{m}$ there exists a stationary monetary equilibrium with prices $q=-z(1)/\bar{m}$ and $\pi^t=1$, t=1,2,... . Further, this stationary equilibrium is unstable.

Proof.- From the budget constraint $1 \cdot z(1)+x(1)=0$. Hence, for $\pi^t=1$ we shall have equilibrium for periods t=2,3, ... By Proposition III.1 , the assumption that $\bar{\pi}<1$ implies that $z(1)<0$. Therefore, $q=-z(1)/\bar{m}>0$ and clears the markets at period t=1. Hence, this is a monetary equilibrium.

In order to prove the unstability of this monetary equilibrium we shall evaluate $d\pi^{t+1}/d\pi^t$ at the equilibrium prices $\pi^t=1$. From (IV.6) we can obtain that

$$d\pi^{t+1}/d\pi^{t} = 1 + [z(1)/z'(1)].$$

Hence, the fact that $z(1)<0$ (for $\pi<1$) and the assumption that $\partial z^{t}/\partial p(t)<0$ establish that $d\pi^{t+1}/d\pi^{t}>1$ and thus that this stationary equilibrium is unstable. QED.

Propositions IV.2 and IV.4 together imply that for stationary economies the inefficiency of the barter equilibrium is the necessary and sufficient condition for the existence of monetary equilibria. Further, as we shall see in Proposition IV.6, one of these monetary equilibria is Pareto optimal. This result was proven by David Gale [27] and more recently by Mitra [45] for the case of "active" monetary policies with the stock of money varying through time. It must be pointed out that this result is specific of stationary economies. Okuno and Zilcha [48] have provided an example of a non-stationary economy (but assymptotically stationary) in which there exists no monetary equilibrium in spite of the fact that the walrasian equilibrium is inefficient. Moreover, Cass, Okuno and Zilcha [47] have shown that with many (and different) agents in each generation we may have that barter and monetary equilibria are both Pareto optimal and cases in which are both inefficient.

In monetary equilibria consumers can bring into effect demands that diverge from walrasian allocations. For every agent t the value of his divergence is $-p(t)z^{t}(\pi^{t})=q\,\bar{m}$ .Therefore a competitive equilibrium is monetary if and only if the aggregate present value of the divergences with respect to the walrasian allocation is infinite, i.e. $\Sigma\text{-}p(t)z^t(\pi^t)=+\infty$. For some monetary equilibria these unbounded divergences in value may be associated with real divergences that become insignificant, in other words, whose aggregate real value is finite $\Sigma\text{-}z^t(\pi^t)<+\infty$. It seems natural to call these equilibria "weakly monetary" and use the word "strongly monetary" for those equilibria whose aggregate real divergence is unbounded, $\Sigma\text{-}z^t(\pi^t)=+\infty$.

The monetary equilibrium that we have shown to exist in Proposition IV.4 is of the latter kind. Further, we shall now show that this is the unique strongly monetary equilibrium and that there is a continuum of weakly monetary equilibria.

Proposition IV.5 Let a stationary Overlapping Generations economy have a walrasian equilibrium not Pareto optimal, i.e. $\bar{\pi}<1$. Then for a stock of money $\bar{m}$, there exists a unique strong monetary equilibrium with prices $q=-z(1)/\bar{m}$ and $\pi^t=1$, $t=1,2,\ldots$. Further, there is a continuum of weakly monetary equilibria.

Proof.- Let us consider in the first place equilibria with $\hat{q}>-z(1)/\bar{m}$. Since by assumption z is decreasing in π, $\hat{\pi}>1$. In Proposition IV.3 we have shown that $\pi=1$ is an unstable stationary equilibrium. Therefore, for some finite T we shall have that $\hat{\pi}^t \geqq 1+\delta$, $t \geqq T$ and $\delta>0$. From this it follows that $p(t)=\Pi^{t-1}(1/\hat{\pi}^r)<(1+\delta)^{-(t-1)}$ and therefore $\text{Lim inf}_{t\to\infty} p(t) = 0$. But, from Proposition IV.2, this would violate a necessary condition for the existence of a monetary equilibrium.

Let us now consider $\tilde{q} < -z(1)/\bar{m}$. We then shall have that $\bar{\pi} \leqq \tilde{\pi}^1 < 1$. Because of the unstability of equilibrium paths at the neighbourhood of $\pi=1$, we have that for some finite T we shall have that $\tilde{\pi}^t \leqq 1-\delta < 1$, $t \geqq T$ and $\delta > 0$. Therefore for some $T' > T$ we have that

(IV.7) $$\Pi^{t-1} \tilde{\pi}^r \leqq (1-\delta)^{t-1}, \text{ for } t \geqq T'.$$

Equilibrium in the money market requires that

$$-z(\tilde{\pi}^t) = \tilde{q}\,\bar{m}/\tilde{p}(t) = \tilde{q}\,\bar{m}\,\Pi^{t-1}\,\tilde{\pi}^r,\ t=1,2,...$$

and therefore

$$-\Sigma\, z(\tilde{\pi}^t) = \Sigma\, \tilde{q}\,\bar{m}/\tilde{p}(t) = \Sigma\, \tilde{q}\,\bar{m}\,\Pi^{t-1}\,\tilde{\pi}^r.$$

But from inequality (IV.7), $\Sigma\, \tilde{q}\,\bar{m}\,\Pi^{t-1}\,\tilde{\pi}^r$ converges because $\Sigma\,(1-\delta)^t$ converges for $\delta > 0$. Therefore, $\tilde{q}$ and $\tilde{\pi}$ correspond to a weakly monetary equilibrium. QED.

We have so far shown the existence of strong and weakly monetary equilibria and that this is related to the inefficiency of the walrasian equilibrium. We shall now demonstrate that when monetary equilibria exist there is at least one that is Pareto optimal. This, together with Proposition III.4 , shows that there always exist efficient competitive equilibria, either walrasian or monetary.

Proposition IV.6 In a stationary Overlapping Generations economy there always exists at least one Pareto optimum competitive equilibrium.

Proof.- In Proposition III.4 we have shown the existence of a competitive, walrasian equilibrium which may or may not be Pareto optimal. Suppose that this equilibrium allocation is not Pareto optimal. In that case, from Proposition IV.5, we know that there exists a strong monetary equilibrium. By definition we have that for a strong monetary equilibrium

$$\Sigma -z(\pi^t) = q\ \overline{m}\ \Sigma 1/p(t) \quad = +\infty.$$

Therefore, by Proposition II.5 this equilibrium is Pareto optimal. Hence, either the walrasian equilibrium is Pareto efficient or there exists a strong monetary, Pareto efficient equilibrium. QED.

From the previous Proposition it is clear that fiat money is a very useful devise which permits economies to achieve fully efficient allocations when the market mechanism is insufficient to bring about Pareto optimal outcomes. But let us now look at the role of money from a slightly different angle. In an Arrow-Debreu description of an economy, the Second Fundamental Theorem of Welfare Economics tells us that every efficient allocation can be achieved as a competitive equilibrium after an appropriate redistribution of individual endowments, or following Pigou by means of lump-sum taxes and transfers. In general, when society is not satisfied with the competitive outcome associated with the *status quo* , it can produce alternative consumption allocations by taking away resources of some agents and giving resources to other agents. The remarkable characteristic of fiat money in Overlapping Generations economies is that without altering the individual distribution of ownership over the initial resources, the government can induce a different equilibrium consumption allocation by issuing a number of intrinsically worthless pieces of paper. As shown in Proposition IV.5 it is possible to generate a continuum of different consumption allocations as monetary equilibria for a given distribution of individual endowments.

Of course, by issuing a number of notes at period t=1 the government cannot implement any weakly Pareto optimal consumption allocation. As a matter of fact, the monetary equilibria turn out to be independent of the number of paper notes issued. At this point two questions emerge quite naturally. The first question to study comes from the observation that there is nothing preventing the governement from issuing additional money in subsequent periods. Very little work has been done in the area of "active" monetary policies. Most of the literature [5] concentrates on policies in which the government can withdraw as well as add money to the economy : the so-called "tax-transfer" policies. These policies thus involve the transfer of money to some agents (which will raise his income, unless we have a "transfer paradox") and the taxation (in income) of other agents, or generations. Without denying the applied relevance of such a rich class of policies, from the theoretical point of view followed here it is more interesting to examine the outcomes of policies consisting of transfers only[6]. But this question has not been fully answered yet. The second problem worth studying is whether or not every weakly efficient allocation can be implemented as a monetary equilibrium, possibly with some redistribution of endowments. One can imagine that eventhough a full redistribution of endowments may not be possible, a partial redistribution accompanied by an appropriate monetary policy might be powerful enough as to enable the government to implement as a monetary equilibrium any target consumption allocation. This question is answered in Chapter VI, Proposition VI.13, for the case of "passive" monetary policies with a single monetary injection at t=1.

IV.4. Comments on Monetary Equilibria with Many Commodities

In the previous section we have pointed to the fact that the introduction of fiat money may help the competitive mechanism in bringing about efficiency. We shall devote this section to giving an intuitive explanation of this property.

The existence of fiat money allows agents to transfer purchasing power from present to future. As depicted in Figure IV.3, consumers can choose a consumption bundle away from the value of their first period resources by an amount $\overline{m}$ and transfer this amount of fiat money into the second period of his life, when it will be purchased by agents of the new generation.

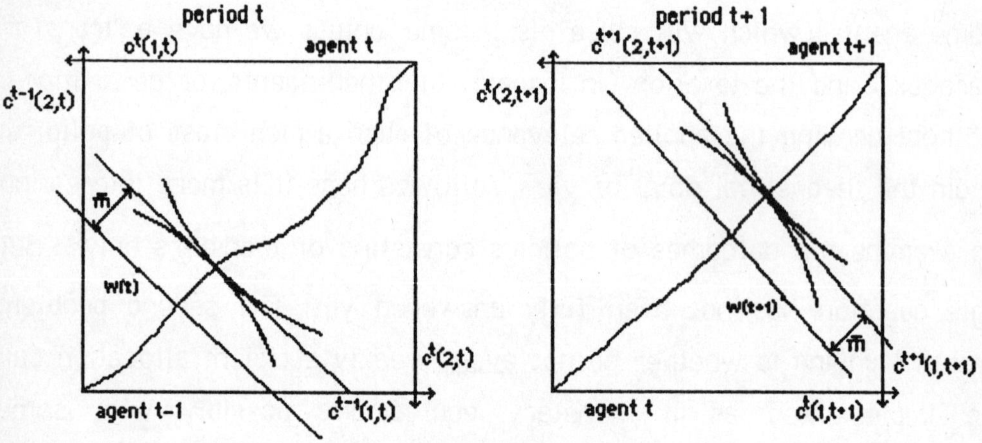

Figure IV.3

There are no general results about the existence of an

efffficent competitive equilibrium for monetary economies with many commodities [8]. Cass, Okuno and Zilcha [12] made it plain that the results obtained for the simple one-good stationary economy, as in David Gale [27], were not robust. They showed that there exist non-stationary economies for which the inefficiency of the Walrasian equilibrium is not sufficient for the existence of an efficient monetary equilibrium. Fot he many commodities case, Benveniste and Cass [8] consider a stationary environment of endowments and preferences and one consumer per generation. Further, inidividual preferences are assumed to be intertemporally separable. Under these assumptions, they show that the ineffeciency of the barter,Walrasian equilibrium is a sufficient condition for the existence of an efficient monetary equilibrium with a fixed stock of fiat money. This result has been generalized in Esteban, Mitra and Ray [26] for the class of "active" monetary policies, with a varying stock of fiat money.

We shall now sketch the main arguments in Esteban, Mitra and Ray [26]. The nature of problem of consumer choice does not change much with the introduction of many commodities per period. However, it may be useful to put forward some minor remarks in reference to the form of the budget constraints in the absence of money acting as a store of value. Specifically, when fiat money is available agents maximize subject to a single, lifetime budget constraint, whereas without money agents face a sequence of budget constraints.

With a single budget constraint a typical consumer solves

$$\text{Max } u^t(c^t(t),c^t(t+1)) \qquad \text{subject to}$$

$$p(t)w^t(t)+p(t+1)w^t(t+1)=y^t(t)+y^t(t+1)\geqq p(t)c^t(t)+p(t+1)c^t(t+1),$$

where $y^t(t)$ and $y^t(t+1)$ stand for the "income" of agent t in periods t and t+1.

We can now consider the following question : if we substract one unit from the income in period t, how much should we compensate that concumer for in t+1 to leave his utility unchanged?. The answer is trivial : one unit.

Let us now consider the case in which the futures markets are inactive, possibly due to the overlapping structure of the population of consumers. Individual agents then face a sequence of two one-period budget constraints. The restricted maximization problem now is

$$\text{Max } u^t(c^t(t),c^t(t+1)) \qquad \text{subject to}$$

$$p(t)w^t(t)=y^t(t)\geqq p(t)c^t(t) \text{ and}$$

$$p(t+1)w^t(t+1)=y^t(t+1)\geqq p(t+1)c^t(t+1).$$

Since we have now two budget constraints we have too the two associated Lagrange multipliers $\lambda^t(t)$ and $\lambda^t(t+1)$, which can be interpreted as the marginal utility of income in each period. If we now consider the previous question, the answer would be that for a change of size $dy^t(t)$ we need to compensate for with a change $dy^t(t+1)$ satisfying

$$\lambda^t(t)\, dy^t(t) + \lambda^t(t+1)\, dy^t(t+1) = 0.$$

Therefore, unless $\lambda^t(t)=\lambda^t(t+1)$ agents will experience a utility loss in the absence of operative future markets. When $\lambda^t(t)>\lambda^t(t+1)$, individuals would prefer to transfer future resources to the present, i.e. agents would like to borrow when young. When $\lambda^t(t)<\lambda^t(t+1)$ agents would prefer to save when young and transfer purchasing power to their old age. The introduction of money or any store of value can provide a remedy for inefficiencies of this latter sign. The first type of inefficiency would require instead a social institution operating as "negative" money. It is clear that when the possibility of "transfer paradoxes" has been ruled out, the introduction of "negative" money cannot bring about a Pareto improvement. The first generation would always be worse-off. Therefore, let us examine whether the fact that $\lambda^t(t)<\lambda^t(t+1)$ at the Walrasian equilibrium is relevant information for the existence of a Pareto optimal monetary equilibrium.

We shall examine here the simplest possible model for economies with many commodities. Following Benveniste and Cass [8] we shall consider an environment stationary in endowments and preferences and with one consumer per generation. Individual preferences will be assumed to be intertemporally separable. Further, and in order to keep things simple, we shall assume that the economy satisfies the properties granting a unique Walrasian equilibrium, as discussed in section III.3.

We shall denote by c^* and p^* the Walrasian consumption allocations and equilibrium prices, respectively. Now, $\lambda^{*t}(t)$ and

$\lambda^{*t}(t+1)$ are the Lagrange multipliers associated with the following constrained maximization problem,

$$\text{Max } u^t(c^t(t),c^t(t+1)) \qquad \text{subject to}$$

$$p^{*s}(t)w^t(t) \geqq p^{*s}(t)c^t(t) \text{ and}$$

$$p^{*s}(t+1)w^t(t+1) \geqq p^{*s}(t+1)c^t(t+1),$$

where $p^{*s}(t)$ is the scalar projection of $p^*(t)$ on the n-dimensional unit simplex.

Of course, the solution to this problem is $(c^{*t}(t),c^{*t}(t+1))$. It is easy to prove the following proposition. Moreover, because of the stationarity of the economy, $p^{*s}(t)=p^{*s}(t+1)=p^{*s}$, and $c^{*t}(t)=c^{*t+1}(t+1)=c^*(1)$ and $c^{*t}(t+1)=c^{*t+1}(t+2)=c^*(2)$. From this it follows that $\lambda^{*t}(t)=\lambda^{*t+1}(t+1)=\lambda^*(1)$ and $\lambda^{*t}(t+1)=\lambda^{*t+1}(t+2)=\lambda^*(2)$.

Proposition IV.7 The Walrasian equilibrium c^* is inefficient if and only if $\lambda^*(1) < \lambda^*(2)$.

Let us now define an active monetary policy as the sequence $\overline{m}=\{\overline{m}(1),\overline{m}(2),\dots,\overline{m}(t),\dots\}$, with $\overline{m}(t)\geq 0$, t=1,2,... . Since the money stock may increase or decrease, some generations will benefit from net money transfers while some will bear taxes in money, respectively. The general form of the individual maximization problem will be

$$\text{Max } u^0(c^1(1)) \qquad \text{subject to}$$

$$p(1)w^0(1)+q(1)\overline{m}(1) \geqq p(1)c^0(1) \text{ for agent } t=0$$

and for the sequence of agents t=1,2,... we have

$$\text{Max } u^t(c^t(t),c^t(t+1)) \qquad \text{subject to}$$

$$p(t)w^t(t) \geqq p(t)c^t(t)+q(t)m^t \text{ and}$$

$$p(t+1)w^t(t+1)+q(t+1)m^t+q(t+1)[\bar{m}(t+1)-\bar{m}(t)] \geqq p(t+1)c^t(t+1),$$

where m^t is the demand of money of agent t when young, $[\bar{m}(t+1)-\bar{m}(t)]$ represents the transfer or tax that generation has been subject to and $q=\{q(1),q(2),\dots,q(t),\dots\}$ is the sequence of money prices. In a monetary equilibrium, besides the clearing of the commodities markets we shall require the money market to clear as well, that is, $m^t=\bar{m}(t)$, $t=1,2,\dots$.

The previous heuristic arguments capture the essence of the proof of the following propositions by Esteban, Mitra and Ray[26].

Proposition IV.8 Let a monetary policy $\bar{m}$ satisfy:

i) $\text{Lim inf } \bar{m}(t+1)/\bar{m}(t) > 0$;

ii) $\text{Lim sup } \bar{m}(t+1)/\bar{m}(t) < \lambda^*(2)/\lambda^*(1)$; and

iii) $\sum 1/\bar{m}(t) = \infty$.

Then, there exists an efficient monetary equilibrium.

Conditions i) and iii) are necessary for the existence of a monetary equilibrium. Therefore, this theorem tells us how to design examples of monetary policies for which no equilibrium exists.

From the two previous propositions Benveniste and Cass [8] result follows as a corollary. When the Walrasian equilibrium is inefficient we have that $\lambda^*(1)<\lambda^*(2)$. Therefore, a monetary policy consisting in a fixed stock of money satisfies all three conditions stated in Proposition IV.8 and an efficient monetary equilibrium exists.

Notes to Chapter IV

1 A comprehensive presentation of neo-Keynesian monetary theories can be found in Clower [19].

2 The "lack of trust" as analyzed by Douglass Gale [28] and [29] can be considered an explanation for the incompleteness of futures markets. We shall examine Gale's contribution in greater detail later in Chapter V.

3 We are considering here a simple once and for all monetary policy consisting in introducing a number $\bar{m}$ of notes into the economy. Of course, one can think of richer active monetary policies in which money is added or withdrawn in every period. These active policies have been investigated by Balasko and Shell [5] and [7] and Mitra [45].

4 Strictly speaking one can say that agents do not behave competitively any more. They take prices as given, true, but now they are not assumed to believe that at these prices they could tade any desired amount of goods. Consumers do acknowledge that some markets do not operate.

5 The main contributions are due to Balasko and Shell [5] and [7], Mitra [45] and Esteban, Mitra and Ray [25] and [26].

6 This is one of the problems studied by Esteban, Mitra and Ray [25] and [26].

7 The possibility of supporting consumption allocations with prices and active monetary policies has been studied by Balasko and Shell [5] and [7] and Esteban, Mitra and Ray [25] and [26].

8 Millán [44] has proven a theorem of existence of an efficient monetary equilibrium for economies which are assymptotically stationary with many agents per generation, but with one commodity per period.

Part III

The Core in Overlapping Generations Economies

Chapter V A Characterization of the Core

V.1 Introduction

In this Chapter we analyse overlapping generations economies from a game theoretical point of view. Specifically, we shall characterize the core of a pure exchange overlapping generations economy. Since Samuelson's [50] contribution overlapping generations models have been considered as a convenient framework for the analysis of a variety of social institutions which share the common characteristic of permitting intergenerational transfers. Examples of such institutions are fiat money, social security and public debt. By means of the working of these institutions the economy can reach Pareto optimal consumption allocations which would not be accessible with the standard institutional framework implicit in the Arrow-Debreu model. The problem we wish to study is whether these institutions are socially stable, i e. will not be refused by some agents.

Douglas Gale [28] and [29] has recently analysed a similar problem. He was the first to point out a particular type of social instability which arises in intertemporal models due to the lack of trust in the fulfilment of trade contracts concerning goods to be delivered at different dates. Using a finite horizon pure exchange model, Gale justifies the lack of trust on some allocations by the inherent incentives to break the futures contracts when the time of the delayed delivery comes.

In our case, we too have a problem of lack of trust on the viability of some consumption allocations. However, and due to the infinite string of overlapping generations, the lack of confidence arises not because agents may break contracts signed by themselves (as in Gale), but because they are aware that some contracts might be unacceptable to the still unborn generations. In other words, the social viability of the institutions associated with intergenerational transfers requires that every agent has the certainty that such institutions will be accepted by the generations to come.

It is our purpose to examine this problem by means of the notion of core. This notion has already been used in overlapping generations economies by Hendricks et al. [36], Kovenock [43], Chae [16] and Chae and Esteban [17]. Nevertheless, it might be useful to justify the use of a cooperative approach in a model in which agents come in an infinite sequence through time. Indeed it is hard to imagine how agents living in unconnected periods can meet and agree on forming a coalition. However, and in spite of the fact that actual bargaining can take place only among agents of coexisting generations, fully informed, rational consumers will behave as if such coalitions could be formed. The sequential structure of the overlapping generations model requires that only those allocations acceptable for all unborn generations can be acceptable for agents belonging to two coexisting generations. It is in this sense that we can talk of coalitions.

The most significant result of this Chapter is the complete characterization of the consumption allocations which belong to the core of the economy. From this characterization it will be clear that the set of core allocations might be empty for some economies. This is the case of one-good exchange economies when the initial endowments allocation is not Pareto optimal. This example of an empty core is of a particular relevance because important contributions to modern monetary theory have been made using the one-good overlapping generations model.

The structure of this Chapter is as follows. In section V.2 we describe the essential elements of the model and introduce the main assumptions. The next section is devoted to the notions of intertemporal efficiency proposed by Balasko and Shell [4] and to the crucial concept of sequential individual rationality. Section V.4 considers the bargaining problem and gives the formal definitions of blocking coalitions and core of the economy. The main propositions of this chapter are presented in Section V.5. We demonstrate that with intertemporal separability of individual preferences Pareto optimality and sequential individual rationality are necessary and sufficient conditions for a consumption allocation to belong to the core. In the next section we examine the problem of existence and give examples of empty and non-empty cores. We prove that, given the aggregate endowments, for any Pareto optimal consumption allocation there exist individual distributions of the initial endowments for which that consumption allocation is either in the core or outside the core. Finally, in Section V.7, we conclude the chapter by discussing the robustness of our results with respect to alternative specifications of the model and/or of the notion of core.

V.2. The model

In our research we shall closely follow the specification of a pure exchange overlapping generations economy laid down by Balasko and Shell [4]. In this Chapter we shall assume that in every period t, t=1,2,..., one agent is born and lives for two periods. This agent will be denoted by his birth date t. The total population at any point in time is thus constant.

At the beginning of this economy there exists a generation previously born at time $t=0$. In Chapter VII we shall consider economies with many agents per generation.

We shall restrict the analysis to a pure exchange economy with n perishable commodities available at every date. Let $c^t(i,t+s)$ be the consumption of good i $(i=1,2,\dots,n)$ at period $t+s$ $(s=0,1)$ $(t=1,2,\dots)$ by the consumer born at t $(t=0,1,2,\dots)$, $c^t(t+s)\in\mathbb{R}^n_+$ be the consumption vector at period $t+s$ $(s=0,1)$ by the agent born at t, and $c^t\in\mathbb{R}^{2n}_+$ the vector of consumptions corresponding to the two periods that agent will be alive. For generation $t=0$ we have that $c^0=c^0(1)$ and, of course, $c^0\in\mathbb{R}^n_+$. We shall use c to denote the sequence $c=\{c^0,c^1,c^2,\dots\}$. Aggregate consumption at period t will be denoted by $c(t)$, i.e. $c(t)=c^{t-1}(t)+c^t(t)$.

Similarly, we shall let $w^t(i,t+s)$ be the endowment of good i at time $t+s$ of the agent born in period t, $w^t(t+s)\in\mathbb{R}^n_+$ be the endowment vector at period $t+s$ $(s=0,1)$ of the agent born in period t, and $w^t\in\mathbb{R}^{2n}_+$ the vector of endowments corresponding to the two periods that agent will be alive. Again, for generation $t=0$ we have that $w^0=w^0(1)$ and, of course, $w^0\in\mathbb{R}^n_+$. Finally, we shall denote by w the sequence $w=\{w^0,w^1,w^2,\dots\}$. Aggregate endowments at period t will be denoted by $w(t)$, i.e. $w(t)=w^{t-1}(t)+w^t(t)$. Let $\mathbb{W}$ be the set of all sequences w which are uniformly bounded from above.

Preferences of consumer t can be represented by a utility

function $u^t:\mathbb{R}^{2n}_+ \to \mathbb{R}$, for $t=1,2,\ldots$ and $u^0:\mathbb{R}^n_+ \to \mathbb{R}$, for $t=0$.

Assumption V.1 u^t, $t=0,1,2,\ldots$, is strictly increasing in each argument.

We shall later need stronger conditions on individual preferences. Specifically, intertemporal separability will play a prominent role.

Assumption V.2 Utility functions u^t, $t=1,2,\ldots$, are intertemporally separable, i.e. can be written in the form $u^t(c^t)=g^t(v^t_t(c^t(t)),v^t_{t+1}(c^t(t+1)))$, where $g^t:\mathbb{R}^2 \to \mathbb{R}$ and $v^t_{t+s}:\mathbb{R}^n \to \mathbb{R}$, $s=0,1$.

In this economy a consumption allocation is a sequence of consumption vectors specifying the consumption of every consumer at every date. A consumption allocation is thus a sequence $c=\{c^0,c^1,c^2,\ldots\}$ with $c^t \in \mathbb{R}^{2n}_+$. Let **C** be the set of all such sequences.

Definition V.1 A consumption allocation sequence c is <u>feasible</u> if

$$c^{t-1}(t)+c^t(t)=c(t)\leq w^{t-1}(t)+w^t(t)=w(t) \quad \text{for } t=1,2,\ldots .$$

Observe that the fact that there is an infinite string of generations that overlap for one period of their lives makes it possible that in spite of the perishability of goods individuals are not necessarily forced to consume their endowments. Consumption allocations can entail at the individual level a transfer from present to future. This can be done by transfering goods to the previous generation when an agent is in his first period and receiving in the next period a transfer from the then young generation.

V.3 Efficiency and Individual Rationality.

The notion of Pareto optimality needs to be adapted to a model in which there are infinite agents and the possibilities of reallocating goods are limited by the biological fact that each generation only coexists with two other generations, one in each period of his life. We shall follow Balasko and Shell [4] in distinguishing between Pareto optimality and weak Pareto optimality. This distinction tries to reflect the notions of long run and short run dynamic efficiency, respectively. Let us introduce the formal definitions.

Definition V.2 The feasible consumption allocation sequence c is Pareto optimal if there is no $\hat{c}$ such that : i) $\hat{c}$ is feasible; and ii) $u^{j,t}(\hat{c}^{j,t}) \geqq u^{j,t}(c^{j,t})$ for $t=0,1,2,\ldots$, and $j=1,\ldots,m$ with at least one strict inequality.

Definition V.3 The feasible consumption allocation sequence c is weakly Pareto optimal if there is no $\hat{c}$ such that : i) $\hat{c}$ is feasible; ii) $\hat{c}^{j,t} = c^{j,t}$ except for a finite number of periods ; and iii) $u^{j,t}(\hat{c}^{j,t}) \geqq u^{j,t}(c^{j,t})$ for $t=0,1,2,\ldots$, and $j=1,\ldots m$,with at least one strict inequality.

As shown in Chapter II, under the hypothesis that individual utility functions are separable[1] consumption allocations can be depicted as points in a sequence of Edgeworth boxes, one for every period. Weakly Pareto optimal allocations consist of points that belong to the contract curve in every period (see points B in Figure V.1).

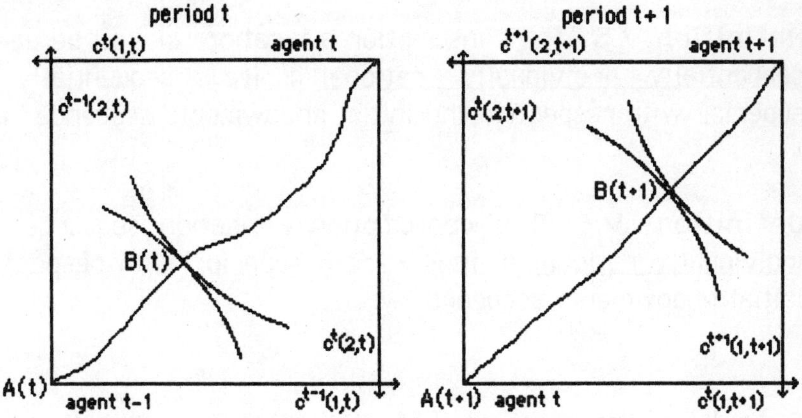

Figure V.1

A necessary condition for a consumption allocation to belong to the core is that the implicit individual exchanges are performed voluntarily, i.e. agents cannot be better-off by refusing to trade. This idea is formalised in the standard notion of "individual rationality". However, when agents live for many periods the decision of accepting or refusing to trade can be taken period by period. Thus, cooperative behaviour in intertemporal economies will require that exchanges are voluntary period per period. We shall call "sequential individual rationality" the intertemporal breakdown of the notion of individual rationality. As we shall see in Propositions V.1 and V.2 sequential individual rationality together with Pareto optimality fully characterize the core allocations.

Definition V.4 A consumption allocation c will be said to be sequentially Pareto superior with respect to allocation $\tilde{c}$ if

i) $u^t(c^t(t),c^t(t+1)) \geqq u^t(\tilde{c}^t(t),c^t(t+1))$, and

ii) $u^t(c^t(t),c^t(t+1)) \geqq u^t(c^t(t),\tilde{c}^t(t+1))$, for $t=1,2,\ldots$ and

$u^o(c^o(1)) \geqq u^o(\tilde{c}^o(1))$.

Definition V.5 The consumption allocation c will be said to be sequentially individually rational if it is sequentially Pareto superior with respect to the initial endowments sequence w.

Definition V.6 The consumption allocation sequence c is individually rational if it is Pareto superior with respect to the initial endowments sequence w.

It is important to note that the fact that the consumption allocation c is sequentially individually rational does not imply that it is individually rational, nor does individual rationality imply sequential individual rationality. Later in the Chapter we shall make use of Assumption V.2. In that case, with intertemporal separability, sequential individual rationality implies individual rationality, but the implication in the reverse sense is false.

V.4 Bargaining in an Ovelapping Generations Economy

Consumption allocations can be viewed as the outcome of quantity bargaining. In this economy only two agents coexist at each period and their resources cannot be transferred from one period to the next. In some respects, this problem looks very much like finding a sequence of solutions to static, temporally unconnected, bargaining problems with two agents and given joint endowments at every date. Yet one of the two agents will survive until the end of the next period and this opens new possibilities to the bargaining problem that are not conceivable in the static analog. More specifically, agent t may obtain from young agent t+1 additional resources if he can persuade him that next period he will in turn be compensated by agent t+2 and so on. This case is the "chocolate bar" example due to Shell [55]. The possibility of such trades is what may prevent competitive barter consumption allocations from being Pareto optimal. This has given rise to the recent body of literature emphasizing the role of fiat money (as a store of value) in implementing Pareto optimal allocations in infinite horizon overlapping generations economies.

Let us assume that there is full information, that is, every agent knows the preferences and endowments of all future generations. A trade proposal from agent 0 to agent 1 consists of a sequence of net trades. The proposed consumption allocation will not be acceptable to agent 1 if there exists a subset of future agents that by forming a coalition can improve upon this allocation. Let agent f be the first member of this blocking coalition. Given full information, agent f-1 would not accept the proposed consumption allocation because he knows that it will not be accepted by agent f. The sequential structure of the model imposes that only those allocations that are acceptable for all unborn generations can be acceptable for any two coexisting agents. The main point is that even though the whole sequence of contracts cannot be "signed" today, any two coexisting rational agents will behave as if these contracts could actually be agreed upon by all agents. It is in this sense that we find it justifiable to talk of "coalitions".

From a game theoretical point of view the overlapping

generations structure of the population is of interest because it constitutes a framework in which the idea of restricted cooperation can be quite naturally applied. Aumann and Drèze [2] and Myerson [46] have studied the case in which coalitions are restricted to some given structures. This assumption fills the gap between full cooperation and no cooperation. In the overlapping generations model the finite lifespan of agents means that agents of any generation t can only bargain with agents of generations t-1 and t+1.

Let us now introduce the formal definitions.

Definition V.7 A <u>coalition</u> is a non-empty connected subset S of the set of all agents.

By the connectedness of S we mean that if $t \in S$ and $t+k \in S$, then $t+r \in S$, $r=1,\ldots,k-1$.

Definition V.8 An allocation $\bar{c}$ is <u>blocked by coalition S</u> if there exists another allocation c such that:

i) c is feasible for coalition S, i.e.

$$c^{t-1}(t) + c^{t}(t) = w^{t-1}(t) + w^{t}(t), \text{ for all } t \in S,$$

ii) $u^t(c^t) \geqq u^t(\bar{c}^t)$ for all agents $t \in S$, with at least one strict inequality for some agent $t \in S$.

Definition V.9 The <u>core</u> of an economy is the set of all allocations that are feasible and not blocked by any coalition.

A coalition will thus be formed by a chain of generations, which might not include all their members. We shall denote by f the first of such generations, i.e. $f=\min\{t/t \in S\}$, and when the number of members of a coalition is finite we shall denote by ℓ the last generation, i.e.

$\ell = \max\{t/t \in S\}$. Taking into account the sequential structure of overlapping generations models and the fact that goods cannot be transferred from one period to the next, the condition that the consumption allocation of a blocking coalition must be feasible for the coalition members, implies that neither the first member of the coalition nor the last one can trade with their neighbouring generations. Thus for any consumption allocation c of a blocking coalition S it must be that

$$c^f = (w^f(f), c^f(f+1)) \text{ and } c^\ell = (c^\ell(\ell), w^\ell(\ell+1)).$$

Initiating or terminating a "chain" coalition is thus equivalent to deciding not to trade with the contemporary agent in one of the two periods every agent is alive. Therefore, the question of whether or not an allocation will be blocked is essentially equivalent to verifying whether it will be worthwhile for any agent to refuse trading with his coexisting agent in view of the gain he can obtain by proposing a new allocation.

V.5 A Characterization of the Core

Consumption allocations that are not Pareto optimal cannot belong to the core because they would be blocked by all the agents in the economy with a Pareto superior consumption allocation. In an overlapping generations economy too Pareto optimality is a necessary condition that must be satisfied by any consumption allocation in the core[2].

In Arrow-Debreu economies not all Pareto optimal allocations belong to the core. Indeed if some agent is left with less utility than when he remains at the initial endowments, he himself will block that consumption allocation. Hence, individual rationality is a necessary property of all core allocations. But as we shall now see sequential individual rationality is also a necessary condition for an allocation to be in the core.

Proposition V.1 Let individual preferences satisfy Assumption V.1 and let $w \in \mathbf{W}$. Let consumption allocation $c \in \mathbf{C}$ belong to the core of the economy. Then, the consumption allocation c satisfies the following properties:

i) Pareto optimality;
ii) Individual rationality; and
iii) sequential individual rationality.

Proof.- Conditions i) and ii) are rather obvious and need no further comments. Let us concentrate on property iii).

Assume that the consumption allocation c does not satisfy property iii), that is, for some agent r we have that either

$$u^r(w^r(r), c^r(r+1)) > u^r(c^r(r), c^r(r+1)) \text{ , or} \tag{V.1}$$

$$u^r(c^r(r), w^r(r+1)) > u^r(c^r(r), c^r(r+1)). \tag{V.2}$$

Let us consider first inequality (V.1). In that case, the coalition formed by all the agents t, $t \geq r$, with the consumption allocation x,

$$x^t = c^t \text{ for all } t \neq r-1, r \text{ ,}$$

$$x^{r-1} = (c^{r-1}(r-1), w^{r-1}(r)) \text{, and}$$

$$x^r = (w^r(r), c^r(r+1))$$

will block allocation c. The blocking consumption allocation x is feasible for the coalition and is strictly prefered by the first member of the coalition. Thus, the consumption allocation c

cannot belong to the core fo the economy.

Consider now inequality (V.2). In such case, the coalition formed by all t, $t \leq r$, with consumption allocation x such that

$$x^t = c^t \text{ for all } t \neq r, r+1,$$

$$x^r = (c^r(r), w^r(r+1)), \text{ and}$$

$$x^{r+1} = (w^{r+1}(r+1), c^{r+1}(r+2))$$

will block consumption allocation c. QED.

From Proposition V.1 the following Corollary is straightforward. [3]

Corollary V.1 Let there be one commodity per period, n=1. Then the core of this economy only contains the initial endowments allocation if it is Pareto optimal, otherwise the core is empty.

Proof.- By Proposition V.1 a consumption allocation is in the core only if it is sequentially individually rational. It is immediate that for n=1, the only feasible allocation that is sequentially individually rational is the initial endowments allocation itself. Further, for n=1, and under Assumption V.1, sequential individual rationality implies individual rationality. Thus the core is empty except when the initial endowments allocation sequence is Pareto optimal. QED.

Corollary V.1 is of some interest because most of the literature analysing the role of money in implementing Pareto optimal allocations has been developed within the framework of one-good overlapping generations models. Our result says that no consumption allocation requiring an intergenerational transfer of commodities will belong to the core. Since money is just the means for implementing such transfer, Corollary V.1 tells us that no monetary equilibrium can be in the core. The relation between competitive equilibria and the core is the object of Chapters VI and VII. In any case, and as we shall see in Chapter VI , with many goods some monetary equilibria can belong to the core.

The intuitive reason why in one good economies no monetary equilibrium belongs to the core is quite straightforward. Every generation finds it advantageous to reject the fiat money carried over by the old generation and start a brand new fiat currency. In doing so they can fully capture for themselves the benefits from printing money. With more than one good per period, for every generation the advantage of printing their own money will have to be weighed against the disadvantage of renouncing to trade with the contemporary generation in one of the two periods of their life. It is that cost what prevents the blocking of all monetary equilibria. In Chapter VI we shall develop this argument in a precise way. Specifically, we shall investigate whether the information revealed by the market, i.e. the price sequence p and the value of M, are sufficient to identify the competitive equilibria which belong to the core.

We can obtain sharper results by introducing stronger assumptions on individual preferences. Specifically, for the remaining of this Chapter we shall restrict ourselves to utility functions that are weakly separable in the consumption bundles of the two periods, i.e. satisfy Assumption V.2 concerning intertemporal separability of preferences. While in Proposition V.1 we have given necessary conditions for an allocation to belong to the core, in Proposition V.2, and under

Assumptions V.1 and V.2 we shall obtain necessary and sufficient conditions.

Proposition V.2 Let preferences satisfy Assumptions V.1 and V.2 and let $w \in \mathbf{W}$ be the sequence of initial endowments. A consumption allocation sequence $c \in \mathbf{C}$ belongs to the core if and only if it is Pareto optimal and sequentially individually rational.

Proof.- We need only to concentrate on sequential individual rationality. That this property is a necessary condition has already been established in Proposition V.1. Let us prove sufficiency.

We can start by noting that under Assumption V.2 all sequentially individually rational allocations are also individually rational. Let us now consider a consumption allocation c that is Pareto optimal and sequentially individually rational. Assume that there is a coalition S with a consumption allocation x blocking c. Let f be the first member of this blocking coalition. Since the consumption allocation c is sequentially individually rational we have that

$$u^f(c^f(f),c^f(f+1)) \geqq u^f(w^f(f),c^f(f+1)).$$

Being the first member of the blocking coalition S, the following inequality must hold

$$u^f(w^f(f),x^f(f+1)) > u^f(c^f(f),c^f(f+1)).$$

By Assumptions V.1 and V.2, these two inequalities imply the following inequalities

$$u^f(c^f(f),x^f(f+1)) > u^f(w^f(f),x^f(f+1)) > u^f(c^f(f),c^f(f+1)).$$

Let us consider in the first place the case in which the blocking coalition S is formed by an infinite number of agents. Then, allocation y such that

$$y^t = c^t \text{ for all } t<f,$$

$$y^f = (c^f(f),x^f(f+1)), \text{ and}$$

$$y^t = x^t \text{ for all } t>f,$$

is feasible and $u^t(y^t) \geqq u^t(c^t)$ with strict inequality for at least agent f. But this contradicts the assumption that c is Pareto optimal.

Let us consider now the case of a blocking coalition with a finite number of agents. Following the same steps as before, we have for the last member ℓ of the blocking coalition the following inequalities

$$u^\ell(x^\ell(\ell),c^\ell(\ell+1)) \geqq u^\ell(x^\ell(\ell),w^\ell(\ell+1)) \geqq u^\ell(c^\ell(\ell),c^\ell(\ell+1)).$$

Thus, the consumption allocation y such that

$$y^t = c^t \quad \text{for all } t<f \text{ and all } t>\ell,$$

$$y^t = x^t \quad \text{for all } t,\ f < t < \ell,$$

$$y^t = (c^f(f),x^f(f+1)), \text{ and}$$

$$y^\ell = (x^\ell(\ell),c^\ell(\ell+1)),$$

is feasible and $u^t(y^t) \geqq u^t(c^t)$ with strict inequality for at least agent f . We obtain again a contradiction with the hypothesis that c is Pareto optimal. QED.

In Figure V.2 we give an illustration of Proposition V.2. We assume n=2 and strictly quasi-concave intra-period utility functions. The shaded

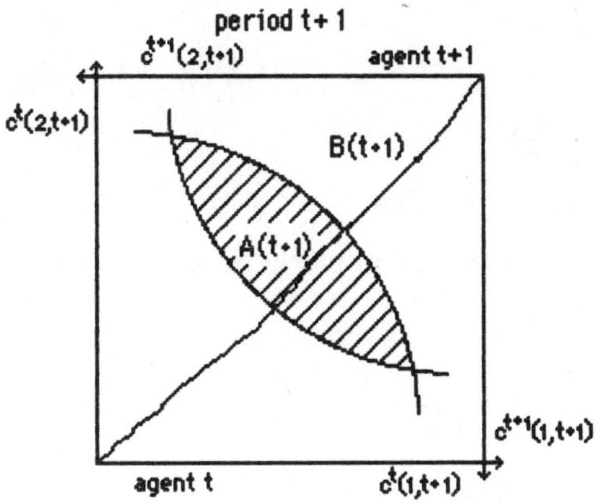

Figure V.2

area shows the consumption allocations that are sequentially individually rational in period t+1. Balasko and Shell [4] have proven that all Pareto optimum consumption allocations are weakly Pareto optimal. Thus, Pareto optimal consumption allocations must be on the intra-period contract curve of the corresponding Edgeworth box. Assuming that points A and B correspond to two alternative Pareto optimum consumption allocations sequence, the consumption allocation B would not be in the core. In order to verify whether the consumption allocation A belongs to the core we should construct the full sequence of Edgeworth boxes and check that the sequence of points A are in the shaded area in every period.

V.6 The Existence of Core Allocations

In the previous section we have obtained the necessary and sufficient conditions for a consumption allocation to belong to the core of the economy, namely: Pareto optimality and sequential individual rationality. Yet we have said nothing as to whether or not the set of core allocations is empty. It is clear that a consumption allocation is in the core if it belongs to the intersection of the set of Pareto optimal allocations and the set of sequentially individually rational allocations. However, we are not in a position to give a full answer to the question about the existence of core allocations. The main difficulty is that we know very little about the structure of the set of Pareto optimal allocations in overlapping generations economies[4] and nothing about the set of sequentially individually rational consumption allocations.

In this section we shall not attempt to give a general proof of existence of core allocations. We shall simply show that the concepts of Pareto optimality and sequential individual rationality are neither mutually exclusive nor does one make the other redundant. As we shall demonstrate the two concepts are quite independent. We have proven in Section V.6 that for $n=1$, economies in which the initial endowments are not Pareto optimal have an empty core. We shall now see that the existence of empty cores is by no means specific to economies with one good. We shall give examples of economies with an empty core and examples of economies with a non-empty core.

Whether a consumption allocation is Pareto optimal or not does not depend on the individual distribution of initital endowments. Therefore, we need only to specify individual preferences and the aggregate endowments in every period. In this section we shall consider economies with given preferences and aggregate endowments and then vary the individual distribution of endowments between the two agents that are alive in every period. Therefore, while the set of Pareto optimal consumption allocations will remain unmodified we shall change the set of sequential individual rational allocations. In this way we shall produce empty and non-empty intersections of the two sets.

Let us denote by $\overline{w}(t)$ the aggregate endowments available at period t and by $\overline{w}$ the sequence $\overline{w} = \{\overline{w}(1), \overline{w}(2), \dots\}$. Since $w \in \mathbf{W}$ it is obvious that $\overline{w} \in \mathbf{W}$ as well. Given a sequence of aggregate endowments $\overline{w}$, we shall denote by $W(\overline{w})$ the set of sequences of individual initial endowments such that

$$w^{t-1}(t)+w^t(t)=\overline{w}^t\ ,\quad w^{t-s}(t)\in\mathbb{R}^n_+,\ s=0,1 \text{ and } t=1,2,\dots\ .$$

Let $C(\overline{w})$ be the set of consumption allocations sequences satisfying:

i) $c^{t-1}(t)+c^t(t)=\overline{w}^t$, $t=1,2,\dots$; and

ii) c^t is uniformly bounded below by a strictly positive vector y, $y\in\mathbb{R}^{2n}_{++}$, $t=1,2,\dots$.

Therefore, a consumption allocation sequence c, $c\in C(\overline{w})$, is feasible and belongs to the strict interior of the Edgeworth box for every period t, $t=1,2,\dots$.

Let us consider an economy such that Pareto optimal allocations exist and that at least one Pareto optimal consumption allocation sequence $\bar{c}$ belongs to the set $C(\bar{w})$, i.e. $\bar{c} \in C(\bar{w})$. We shall first give an example of an economy in which the set of core allocations is empty.

Empty core

Balasko and Shell [4] have proven that whilst all Pareto optimal consumption allocations are weakly Pareto optimal, the converse is false, i.e. that not all weakly Pareto optimal allocations are Pareto optimal. Let us consider now a weakly Pareto optimal consumption allocation sequence $\tilde{c}$, $\tilde{c} \in C(\bar{w})$ that is not Pareto optimal. Then, for the initial endowments sequence such that $w(t) = \tilde{c}(t)$, $t=1,2,\ldots$, the core is empty. From Definition V.5 it is immediate that in this case the set of sequentially individually rational consumption allocations contains one element only, namely, the initial endowments sequence itself. But, by assumption this consumption allocation is not Pareto optimal and hence the core is empty.

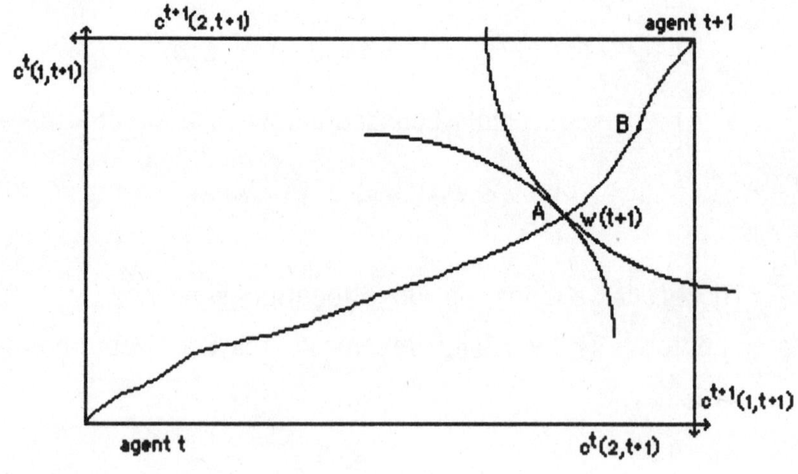

Figure V.3

Pareto optimal consumption sequence $\bar{c} \in C(\bar{w})$. We have a trivial example of an endowment sequence w such that the core is non-empty. This is the case of the endowments allocation sequence w such that $w(t) = \bar{c}(t)$ for $t=1,2,\ldots$. Indeed in that case $\bar{c}$ is sequentially individually rational by construction and Pareto optimal by assumption. Therefore $\bar{c}$ is in the core of the economy.

Let us now consider the set $W(\bar{c})$ of all the initial endowments sequences w such that:

i) $w \in W(\bar{w})$; and

ii) $v^{t-1}{}_t(w^{t-1}(t)) \leqq v^{t-1}{}_t(\bar{c}^{t-1}(t))$ and

$v^t{}_t(w^t(t)) \leqq v^{t-1}{}_t(\bar{c}^t(t))$, $t=1,2,\ldots$.

Since $\bar{c} \in C(\bar{w})$, and making the additional assumption that preferences are strictly quasi-concave, the set $W(\bar{c})$ will have more than one element. This corresponds to the shaded area of Figure V.4 . Given a Pareto optimal consumption allocation sequence $\bar{c}$, the set $W(\bar{c})$ contains all the initial endowments sequences w for which $\bar{c}$ belongs to the core of the economy.

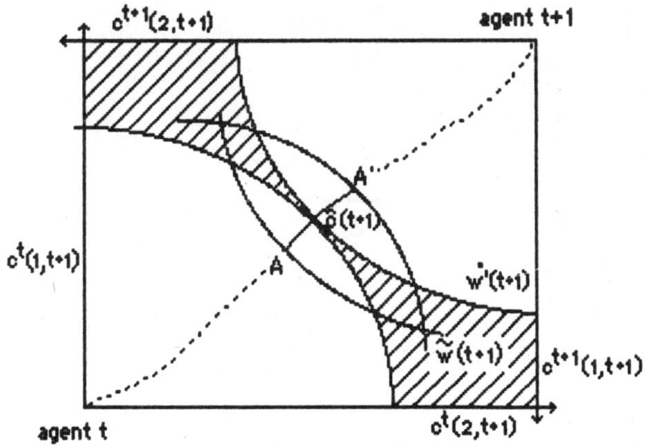

Figure V.4

Let the endowments allocation sequence $w \in W(\bar{c})$. Then, by construction, $\bar{c}$ is sequentially individually rational and Pareto optimal, and thus in the core. Moreover, since $\bar{c} \in C(\bar{w})$, and by the strict quasi-concavity of individual preferences, there exist endowment sequences $\tilde{w} \in W(\bar{c})$ such that

$$v^{t-1}{}_t(\bar{c}^{t-1}(t)) \geq v^{t-1}{}_t(\tilde{w}^{t-1}(t)) \text{ and}$$

$$v^t{}_t(\bar{c}^t(t)) \geq v^t{}_t(\tilde{w}^t(t)) \text{ ,for } t = 1,2,...$$

with strict inequality for at least some finite number of agents.

We can summarize the contents of this section in the following Proposition.

Proposition V.3 Let $\bar{w}$ be a sequence of aggregate endowment allocations such that $\bar{w} \in \mathbf{W}$. Assume that Pareto optimal consumption allocations exist and at least one Pareto optimal consumption sequence $\bar{c} \in C(\bar{w})$. Then, there exist distributions of individual endowments $\tilde{w}$ and $\bar{w}$, $\tilde{w} \in W(\bar{w})$ and $\bar{w} \in W(\bar{w})$, such that:

i) for $\tilde{w}$ the set of core allocations is empty, and

ii) for $\bar{w}$ the set of core allocations is non-empty.

Proof.- Trivial from the foregoing discussion.

A general characterization of the competitive equilibrium consumption allocations that belong to the core of the economy is given in Chapters VI and VII.

V.7 Final Remarks

In this Chapter we have examined the core of an overlapping generations economy and have shown that a consumption allocation belongs to the core if and only if it is Pareto optimal and sequentially individually rational. We wish now to focus on the fact that the set of core allocations might be empty. This point is of relevance since we risk having defined a vacuus concept. Let us now discuss why the set of core allocations is "small" and whether there exist obvious alternative concepts not yielding empty sets.

One may think that the core is small in the economy we have described because each period is essentially unconnected with the colateral periods. Indeed, goods are perishable and the consumption allocation arrived at in any date t imposes no physical restrictions on the consumptions allocations that can be agreed upon at any future date. Moreover, since individual utility functions are intertemporally separable, today's agreements have no influence on the utility level that can be obtained tomorrow. Let us briefly examine the possibility of enlarging the core by diminishing this independence between periods. An obvious way of establishing links across periods is dropping Assumption V.2, i.e. intertemporal separability of utility functions. Yet, we have proven in Proposition V.1 that sequential individual rationality is a necessary condition for belonging to the core. Therefore, dispensing with Assumption V.2 will not give a larger core. The core will be a subset of the intersection of the Pareto optimal set with the set of sequentially individually rational allocations. Another possibility of strengthening the connection between periods is eliminating the assumption that goods are perishable. Under non-perishability, the main difference is that stocks can be carried over from one period to the next. Let us consider a given period t . Agent t-1's resources may now be larger than his current endowments, but this is indistiguishable from the case in which agent t-1 has more endowments when old. As for agent t , the possibility of storing may reduce, but never increase the implicit losses associated with blocking. Thus, the core cannot be larger than under perishability. Since the essential point is making cooperation between individuals of different generations indispensible, it would be interesting to explore the case of productive economies in which some input (e.g. capital goods) are owned by the old generation and some (e.g. labour) by the young one.

Besides changes in the specification of the model one may think that the core is not an appropriate concept for overlapping generations economies. On this respect the only alternative concept available in the overlapping generations literature is the bounded core (and the closely related concept of the short run core)[5]. Hendricks et al. [36] have shown that in one good economies if only finite member coalitions are allowed the (bounded) core consists of the initial endowments allocation. Therefore, all walrasian equilibria belong to the (bounded) core[6]. It is easy to see that for n-goods economies the bounded core would contain all the consumption allocation sequences that are weakly Pareto optimal and sequentially individually rational. However, this does not seem to be an interesting substitute concept for the core for at least three reasons. In the first place, I find it difficult to accept that a consumption allocation being Pareto dominated by another one will be considered non-rejectable by rational, non-malevolent agents[7]. The second point worth mentioning is that none of the allocations which are in the bounded core but not in the core is Pareto optimal. Finally, and as a strengthening of this last point, I find it objectionable that the bounded core contains innefficient consumption allocations, i.e. wasteful allocations.

In any case, the fundamental question is the relationship between the core and the set of competitive equilibria. This is the object of Chapters VI and VII. On this point we shall demonstrate that all Pareto optimal walrasian equilibria belong to the core for economies with one agent per generation. For the case of economies with many agents we show that none of the consumption allocations which are implementable (after suitable redistribution of endowments) as monetary equilibria, with either inside, IOU or outside,fiat money, belong to the core as the economy becomes large. Only those allocations that can only be implemented as walrasian equilibria belong to the core of the limit economy.

Notes to Chapter V

[1] The special case of overlapping generations economies with intertemporaly separable preferences has been thoroughly examined by Balasko and Shell [6], Kehoe and Levine [40] and Geanakoplos and Polemarchakis [30].

[2] An alternative approach is that of the bounded core of the economy. This corresponds to the case in which coalitions can contain a finite number of agents only. The obvious implication is that the weakly Pareto optimal consumption allocations not in the core can belong to the bounded core because the infinite coalitions necessary to block non Pareto optimal consumption allocations will then be excluded. The notion of bounded core has been examined by Hendricks et al. [36] and Chae [16] for the Overlapping Generations model , and Kaneko and Wooders [37] and [38] for static models.

[3] This Proposition is due to Hendricks et al. [36].

[4] The main result on this respect is due to Balasko and Shell [5] who demonstrate that the set of Pareto optimal allocations is arc-connected.

[5] See Hendricks et al. [36], Chae [16] and Chae and Esteban [17].

[6] For the case of Overlapping Generations models with discrete time and one agent per generation and one good per period, Hendricks et al. [36] demonstrate that all Walrasian equilibria belong to the bounded core. On the other hand, in an economy with a continuum of agents, Chae [16] proves that the set of Walrasian allocations coincides with the bounded core of the economy.

[7] Balasko and Shell [4, Lemma 5.4] have proven that if a consumption allocation is weakly Pareto optimal and we introduce a modification consisting in utility improving transfers, then if agent t recives a non-zero transfer so does agent $t+1$. Thus, weakly Pareto optimal consumption allocations cannot be blocked by a finite number of agents.

Chapter VI Competitive Equilibria and the Core. One agent per generation

VI.1. Introduction

In Chapter V we identified the necessary and sufficient conditions for a consumption allocation to belong to the core of the economy. However, we have not examined whether the core contains any consumption allocation which can be implemented by means of the competitive mechanism.

In the standard Arrow-Debreu model all competitive equilibria belong to the core of the economy. This property of competitive allocations is essential in providing support for the assumption that agents behave competitively. Indeed, they could not do better by not taking prices as given and reallocating goods among themselves.

In overlapping generations models the competitive assumption does not seem to rest on such firm grounds. As it has been rigorously proven by Kehoe and Levine [40], [41] and [42], Geanakoplos and Polemarchakis [30], and Santos [52] overlapping generations economies will typically display a large number of competitive equilibria. Further, as shown by Santos [52] equilibrium paths can be an n-dimensional manifold, with n goods per period. These results have been used by Grandmont [32] to argue that the rational expectations hypothesis makes little sense in models with indeterminate equilibria.

The results presented in this Chapter are of some relevance for the foundations of the competitive assumption from the point of view of the core of the economy. The fact that the First Fundamental Theorem of Welfare Economics does not apply to overlapping generations economies makes plain that some walrasian allocations will be unanimously rejected by the full sequence of consumers. Therefore, it is obvious that the well known result that the set of competitive equilibria is a subset of the set of core allocations will not be valid here. It is our purpose to study the relationship between competitive equilibria and core in pure exchange overlapping generations economies. On this respect we shall demonstrate that with one agent per generation all Pareto optimal walrasian equilibria belong to the core of the economy[1].

Since Samuelson [50] overlapping generations models have been considered the most appropriate framework for the analysis of monetary equilibria with fiat money. Grandmont [31], Hahn [34],and Kareken and Wallace [39] are examples of books in which money is studied in an overlapping generations model. Indeed one remarkable result is by now common knowledge: that the introduction of an additional good (fiat money) with no intrinsic value can help the economy to attain Pareto optimal allocations. Further, in the competitive monetary equilibrium fiat money will obtain a strictly positive price. But, as we shall see, the fact that in equilibrium fiat money quotes a positive price should not be taken as implying that it will be socially accepted. As a matter of fact, in one good economies no monetary equilibrium belongs to the core of the economy. The results obtained for n-goods economies are quite different. With n-goods some monetary equilibria can be in the core. We demonstrate that in the latter case being or not in the core is a property which depends on the amount of fiat money associated with each equilibrium. Specifically, we obtain a critical upper bound above which monetary equilibria will not be found acceptable, i.e. not in the core.

These results can be given the following interpretation. At first sight, intertemporal economies with one good per period seem to provide a natural model for examining fiat money as a store of value. The essential problem of the intertemporal transfers which cannot be carried out in barter economies appears clearly in one good economies. The extension to economies with n-goods seems more oriented towards modelling the role of money as a means of exchange rather than to providing any additional insight into its role as a store of value. In our case, the social acceptability of fiat money depends not on being a store of value (as the overlapping generations model seems to be designed for) but on being a means of exchange. We prove that with n-goods, what prevents some monetary equilibria from being rejected is the fact that they are accompanied by barter trades with the previous generation. It is the value of such trades which may refrain agents from refusing the existing money and thus from trading with the previous generation.

The purpose of this Chapter is twofold. On the one hand, we shall characterise the competitive equilibria which belong to the core of the economy in terms of equilibrium prices and values of intergenerational transfers relative to the values of intra-generational barter. On the other hand, we shall investigate the existence of equilibria in the core of the economy. We have already mentioned that for economies with one agent per generation all Pareto optimal walrasian allocations belong to the core of the economy. What remains to be demonstrated is that some monetary equilibria do belong to the core. On this respect we prove that for all consumption allocations which can be implemented as a monetary equilibrium there exists a distribution of initial endowments for which that allocation still is a monetary equilibrium and belongs to the core of the economy.

The Chapter is structured as follows. In the next section we introduce the essential notation, definitions and hypotheses. Section VI.3 defines the notion of competitive equilibrium, both walrasian and monetary. In section VI.4 we characterise the competitive equilibria which belong to the core. The existence of competitive allocations in the core is the object of section VI.5. The Chapter ends with a section with concluding remarks.

VI.2. Notation, definitions and assumptions.

We shall assume a pure exchange economy with n perishable commodities available at every date. In every period t, t=1,2,..., one agent is born and lives for two periods. At the beginning of this economy there exists a generation previously born at time t=0. Let $c^t(i,t+s)$ be the consumption of good i (i=1,2,...,n) at period t+s (s=0,1) (t=1,2,...) by the consumer born at t (t=0,1,2,...), $c^t(t+s)\in \mathbb{R}^n_+$ be the consumption vector at period t+s (s=0,1) by the agent born at t, and $c^t \in \mathbb{R}^{2n}_+$ the vector of consumptions corresponding to the two periods that agent will be alive. For generation t=0 we have that $c^0=c^0(1)$ and, of course, $c^0\in \mathbb{R}^n_+$. We shall use c to denote the sequence $c=\{c^0,c^1,c^2,...\}$. Aggregate consumption at period t will be denoted by c(t), i.e. $c(t)=c^{t-1}(t)+c^t(t)$.

Similarly, we shall denote by $w^t(i,t+s)$ the endowment of good i at t+s by the agent born at period t, $w^t(t+s)\in \mathbb{R}^n_+$ be the endowment vector at period t+s (s=0,1) of the agent born at t, and $w^t\in \mathbb{R}^{2n}_+$ the vector of endowments corresponding to the two periods that agent will be alive. Again, for generation t=0 we have that $w^0=w^0(1)$ and, of course, $w^0\in \mathbb{R}^n_+$. Finally, we shall denote by w the sequence $w=\{w^0,w^1,w^2,...\}$.

Aggregate endowments at period t will be denoted by w(t), i.e. $w(t) = w^{t-1} + w^t(t)$. Let $\mathbb{W}$ be the set of all sequences w which are uniformly bounded from above.

Preferences of consumer t can be represented by a utility function $u^t: \mathbb{R}^{2n}_+ \to \mathbb{R}$, for t=1,2,... and $u^0: \mathbb{R}^n_+ \to \mathbb{R}$, for t=0.

Assumption VI.1 u^t, t=0,1,2,... , has strictly positive first order partial derivatives and is strictly quasi-concave.

Assumption VI.2 Utility functions u^t, t=1,2,... , are intertemporally separable, i.e. can be written in the form $u^t(c^t) = g^t(v^t_t(c^t(t)), v^t_{t+1}(c^t(t+1)))$, where $g^t: \mathbb{R}^2 \to \mathbb{R}$ and $v^t_{t+s}: \mathbb{R}^n \to \mathbb{R}$, s=0,1.

We shall take from Balasko and Shell [4] the definitions of Pareto optimality and weak Pareto optimality, reflecting the notions of long run and short run dynamic efficiency, respectively.

Definition VI.1 A consumption allocation sequence c is <u>feasible</u> if

$$c^{t-1}(t) + c^t(t) = c(t) \leqq w^{t-1}(t) + w^t(t) = w(t) \quad \text{for } t=1,2,...$$

Definition VI.2 The feasible consumption allocation sequence c is <u>Pareto optimal</u> if there is no $\hat{c}$ such that : i) $\hat{c}$ is feasible; and ii) $u^{j,t}(\hat{c}^{j,t}) \geqq u^{j,t}(c^{j,t})$ for t=0,1,2,... , and j=1,...,m with at least one strict inequality.

Definition VI.3 The feasible consumption allocation sequence c is weakly Pareto optimal if there is no $\hat{c}$ such that : i) $\hat{c}$ is feasible; ii) $\hat{c}^{j,t} = c^{j,t}$ except for a finite number of periods ; and iii) $u^{j,t}(\hat{c}^{j,t}) \geqq u^{j,t}(c^{j,t})$ for $t=0,1,2,\ldots$, and $j=1,\ldots m$,with at least one strict inequality.

We shall make use of the notions of sequential individual rationality introduced in the previous Chapter.

Definition VI.4 A consumption allocation c will be said to be sequentially Pareto superior with respect to allocation $\tilde{c}$ if

i) $u^t(c^t(t),c^t(t+1)) \geqq u^t(\tilde{c}^t(t),c^t(t+1))$, and

ii) $u^t(c^t(t),c^t(t+1)) \geqq u^t(c^t(t),\tilde{c}^t(t+1))$, for $t=1,2,\ldots$ and

$u^0(c^0(1)) \geqq u^0(\tilde{c}^0(1))$.

Definition VI.5 The consumption allocation c will be said to be sequentially individually rational if it is sequentially Pareto superior with respect to the initial endowments sequence w .

Definition VI.6 The consumption allocation sequence c is individually rational if it is Pareto superior with respect to the initial endowments sequence w.

We shall take from Chapter V the definitions of coalition and core of the economy.

Definition VI.7 A coalition is a non-empty connected subset S of the set of all agents.

By the connectedness of S we mean that if $t \in S$ and $t+k \in S$, then $t+r \in S$, $r=1,\ldots,k-1$.

A coalition will thus be formed by a chain of generations, which might not include all their members. We shall denote by f the first of such generations, i.e. $f=\min\{t/t\in S\}$, and when the number of members of a coalition is finite we shall denote by ℓ the last generation, i.e. $\ell=\max\{t/t\in S\}$.

Definition VI.8 An allocation $\bar{c}$ is blocked by coalition S if there exists another allocation c such that:

i) c is feasible for coalition S, i.e.

$$c^{t-1}(t)+c^{t}(t)=w^{t-1}(t)+w^{t}(t), \text{ for all } t\in S,$$

ii) $u^t(c^t)\geqq u^t(\bar{c}^t)$ for all agents $t\in S$, with at least one strict inequality for some agent $t\in S$.

Definition VI.9 The core of an economy is the set of all allocations that are feasible and not blocked by any coalition.

VI.3. Competitive Equilibria

Full information and perfect foresight is assumed throughout this Chapter. Let $p(i,t)$ denote the price of commodity i delivered at period t, $i=1,\ldots,n$ and $t=1,2,\ldots$, $p(t)$ the vector $(p(1,t),\ldots,p(n,t))\in\mathbb{R}^n_+$, and p the price sequence $p=\{p(1),p(2),\ldots\}$. We shall normalize by setting $p(1,1)=1$ and we shall denote by $\mathbf{P}$ the set of such price sequences, i.e. $\mathbf{P}=\{p/p(1,1)=1, p(t)\in\mathbb{R}^n_+\}$.

Each consumer choses his lifetime consumption pattern by solving the following maximization program

$$\text{Max } u^0(c^0(1)) \qquad \text{subject to}$$

$$p(1)\cdot c^{0}(1) \leqq p(1)\cdot w^{0}(1)+M, \quad \text{where } M \text{ is a finite real number;}$$

and

$$\text{Max } u^t(c^t(t),c^t(t+1)) \qquad \text{subject to}$$

$$p(t)\cdot c^{t}(t)+p(t+1)\cdot c^{t}(t+1) \leqq p(t)\cdot w^{t}(t)+p(t+1)\cdot w^{t}(t+1).$$

We shall denote by $f^t(p(t),p(t+1),w^t)$ the demand vector resulting from agent's t maximization problem. Similarly, $f^0(p(1),w^0,M)$ is the demand vector corresponding to agent $t=0$.

Definition VI.10 A <u>competitive equilibrium</u> is a sequence of commodity prices $p \in \mathbf{P}$, a sequence of initial endowments $w \in \mathbf{W}$ and a consumption allocation sequence c such that:

i) $p(t)\cdot c^t(t) + p(t+1)\cdot c^t(t+1) \leqq p(t)\cdot w^t(t) + p(t+1)\cdot w^t(t+1)$ and $u^t(c^{j,t}) \geqq u^t(\hat{c}^t)$ for all $\hat{c}^t$ satisfying the budget constraint, for $t=1,2,\ldots$, and for $t=0$ $p(1)\cdot c^0(1) \leqq p(1)\cdot w^0(1)+M$ and $u^0(c^0) \geqq u^0(\hat{c}^0)$ for all $\hat{c}^0$ satisfying the budget constraint; and

ii) $c^{t-1}(t) + c^t(t) = w^{t-1}(t) + w^t(t)$ for $t=1,2,\ldots$.

We shall call <u>monetary equilibria</u> those competitive equilibria such that $p(t+1)\cdot(c^t(t+1)-w^t(t+1))=M$, $t=0,1,2,\ldots$ for some $M>0$. The competitive equilibria such that $M=0$ will be called <u>walrasian</u>. Indeed, when $M<0$ consumers will dissave when young and thus will implicitly demand "negative" money. We are not concerned here about the institutional arrangements which could be necessary to implement some consumption allocations. Nevertheless, these equilibria can be obtained as well by means of fiat money, possibly supplemented with money taxes and transfers.

By adding the individual budget constraints and taking into account the market clearing conditions it is easy to obtain that in equilibrium

$$(VI.1)\qquad p(t)\cdot[w^t(t)-c^t(t)]=p(t+1)\cdot[c^{\,t}(t+1)-w^{\,t}(t+1)]=M,\quad t=1,2,\ldots\ .$$

That is, the value of savings when young and the value of dissavings when old are equal and that value remains constant across all generations. We can thus interpret M as the constant nominal value of money purchases (normalised with respect to p(1,1)) associated with this equilibrium. From another point of view we can say that M is the nominal amount of money (i.e. number of physical units times the market price of money) with which we have to endow agent $t=0$ in order to sustain this consumption allocation sequence as a monetary equilibrium, together with the equilibrium price sequence p.

The existence of competitive equilibria has already been proved by Balasko and Shell [4], and [5] and Balasko, Cass and Shell [3], as well as the proposition that competitive allocations are weakly Pareto optimal. In general, for given $w\in\mathbf{W}$ we shall have different equilibria associated with different values of M and price sequences $p\in\mathbf{P}$. Moreover, for $M=0$, there always exists an equilibrium price sequence $p\in\mathbf{P}$ associated with every sequence of endowments $w\in\mathbf{W}$ (Balasko and Shell [4,Proposition 3.10].

Taking into account Assumption VI.2, for a competitive equilibrium M and price sequence p, the sequence of consumption allocations can be obtained from the following maximization program,

(see Figure VI.1)

$$\text{Max } v^t{}_t(c^t(t)) \text{ subject to}$$

$$p(t)\cdot c^{\,t}(t) \leqq p(t)\cdot w^{\,t}(t) - M, \quad \text{for } t=1,2,\dots,$$

and

$$\text{Max } v^t{}_{t+1}(c^t(t+1)) \text{ subject to}$$

$$p(t+1)\cdot c^{\,t}(t+1) \leqq p(t+1)\cdot w^{\,t}(t+1) + M, \quad \text{for } t=0,1,2,\dots .$$

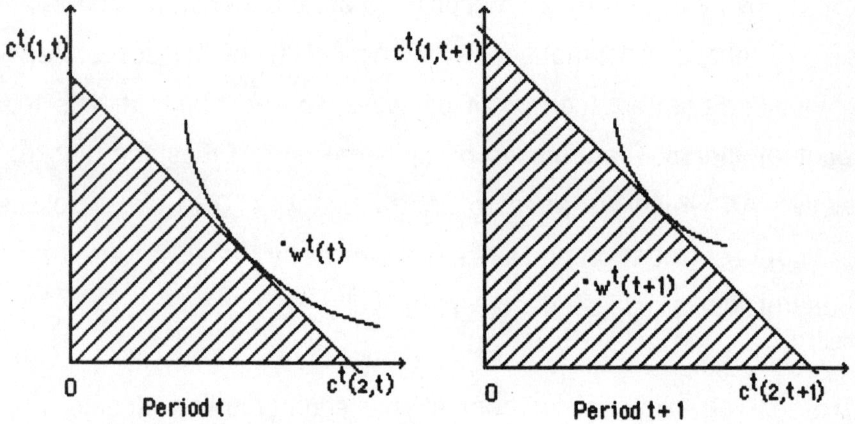

Figure VI.1

Let us note that the indirect utility corresponding to a competitive consumption allocation can thus be expressed as

(VI.2) $$u^t = \varphi^t(h^t{}_t(p(t),p(t)\cdot w^{\,t}(t)-M), h^t{}_{t+1}(p(t+1),p(t+1)\cdot w^{\,t}(t+1)+M)).$$

By Assumption VI.1 $h^t{}_t$ is strictly decreasing and $h^t{}_{t+1}$ strictly decreasing in M.

VI.4. Competitive Equilibria and the Core of the Economy

Corollary V.1 in Chapter V states that for one good economies either the initial endowments belong to the core (if they are Pareto optimal) or the core is empty. From this Corollary V.1 and the definition of monetary equilibrium the following Proposition is immediate.

Proposition VI.1 Let preferences satisfy Assumption 1 and let there be one good per period, n=1. Then no monetary equilibrium belongs to the core.

Proof.- From Corollary V.1 in one good economies no consumption allocation with $c^t \neq w^t$ for some t can belong to the core. Hence, from Definition VI.10 it is immediate that no monetary equilibrium can belong to the core. QED.

Let us now concentrate on monetary equilibria in n-goods economies. Balasko and Shell [4] have provided the characterization of the Pareto optimal allocations in terms of prices. There remain to be characterised the competitive allocations that satisfy sequential individual rationality.

In order to do this, we shall first note that if agent t remains at his initial endowments he obtains a utility level $u^t = g^t(v^t{}_t(w^t(t)), v^t{}_{t+1}(w^t(t+1)))$. Let us consider the following maximization program

$$\text{Max} \quad p(t)\cdot[w^t(t)-c^t(t)] \quad \text{subject to}$$

$$v^t{}_t(c^t(t)) \geqq v^t{}_t(w^t(t)) \text{ , for } t=1,2,\ldots,$$

and

$$\text{Max} \quad p(t+1)\cdot[w^t(t+1)-c^t(t+1)] \quad \text{subject to}$$

$$v^t_{t+1}(c^t(t+1)) \geqq v^t_{t+1}(w^t(t+1)) \text{ , for } t=0,1,2,\ldots \text{ .}$$

Let the solution of this maximization program be the sequence $\bar{c}$. We can now define $b^t(t)$ and $b^t(t+1)$ as

$$b^t(t) = p(t)\cdot[w^t(t)-\bar{c}^t(t)] \quad \text{and}$$

$$b^t(t+1) = p(t+1)\cdot[w^t(t+1)-\bar{c}^t(t+1)].$$

By Assumption VI.1 we have that

$$v^t_{t+s}(w^t(t+s)) = v^t_{t+s}(\bar{c}^t(t+s)) \text{ for } s=0,1 \text{ and } t=1,2,\ldots \text{ ,}$$

$$\text{and } b^t(t+s) \geqq 0 \text{ , } s=0,1 \text{ and } t=0,1,2,\ldots \text{ .}$$

This maximization program is depicted in Figure VI.2, where

$$d^t(t) = b^t(t)/\|p(t)\| \text{ .}$$

The real numbers $b^t(t+s)$, $s=0,1$, are the difference between the minimum expenditure associated with the utility level corresponding to the consumption allocation and the utility of the endowments allocation in every period. These numbers can be interpreted as the maximum amount of income that agent t is willing to pay in order to be allowed access to the market in period $t+s$ at the ruling price sequence p. We shall thus call $b^t(t+s)$ the <u>value of market access</u> for agent t in period $t+s$ at market prices $p(t+s)$, $s=0,1$.

We can now express the utility level associated with the initial endowments as a function of market prices and the value of market access in the periods each agent is alive. Therefore

(VI.3) $u^t=\varphi^t(h^t{}_t(p(t),p(t)w^t(t)-b^t(t)),h^t{}_{t+1}(p(t+1),p(t+1)w^t(t+1)-b^t(t+1)))$.

Figure VI.2

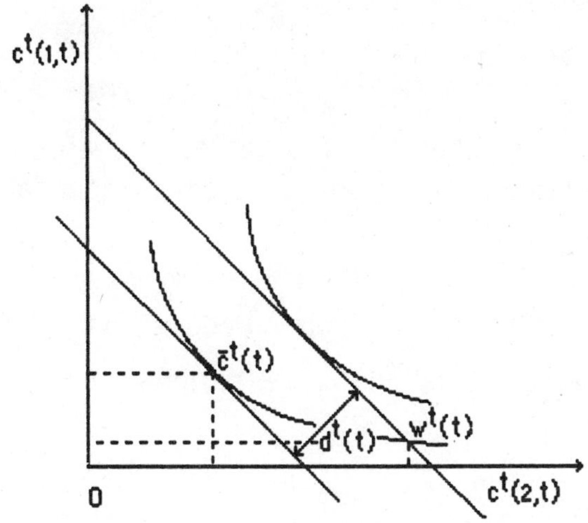

For equilibrium consumption allocation sequences we can restate the definition of sequential individual rationality by means of theindirect utility functions (VI.2) and (VI.3).

Definition VI.5' Let c be an equilibrium consumption sequence relative to the endowment sequence $w\epsilon\mathbf{W}$ with associated equilibrium prices $p\epsilon\mathbf{P}$. Then, allocation c is sequentially individually rational if and only if

i) $M \leq b^t(t)$ for $t=1,2,\ldots$, and

ii) $M \geq -b^t(t+1)$ for $t=0,1,2,\ldots$.

Proposition VI.2 Let preferences satisfy Assumptions VI.1 and VI.2 and let w be the endowment allocation sequence, $w \in \mathbf{W}$ .Then, a Pareto optimal equilibrium consumption allocation sequence c belongs to the core if and only if

$$-b^t(t+1) \leq M \leq b^t(t) \quad \text{for } t=1,2,\ldots$$

where the values of the $b^t(t+s)$, $s=0,1$, have been evaluated at the equilibrium prices and M is the equilibrium nominal purchase of money.

Proof .- Straightforward from Proposition V.2 and the restatement of sequential individual rationality in Definition VI.5'. QED.

Proposition VI.2 puts bounds on the amount of fiat money (positive or negative) associated with core allocations. For the sake of simplicity let us consider Pareto optimal equilibria such that $M>0$. Blocking a consumption allocation can be interpreted as refusing the existing money when young and creating a new currency when the agent is old. Printing new money is equivalent to an increase in the second period nominal income by an amount M. However, when an agent refuses the existing money he is not given access to current market transactions in spot markets, i.e. remains at his initial endowments. He will thus suffer a current loss equivalent to his valuation of the right to market access, $b^t(t)$. Under these circumstances, an agent will have to weigh the current loss $b^t(t)$ against the present value of future gains M. If gains exceed losses the consumption allocation is blocked. This case is depicted in

Figure VI.3, with n=2, where $\mu(t+1)=M/\|p(t+1)\|$ and $d^{t+1}(t+1) = b^{t+1}(t+1)/\|p(t+1)\|$.

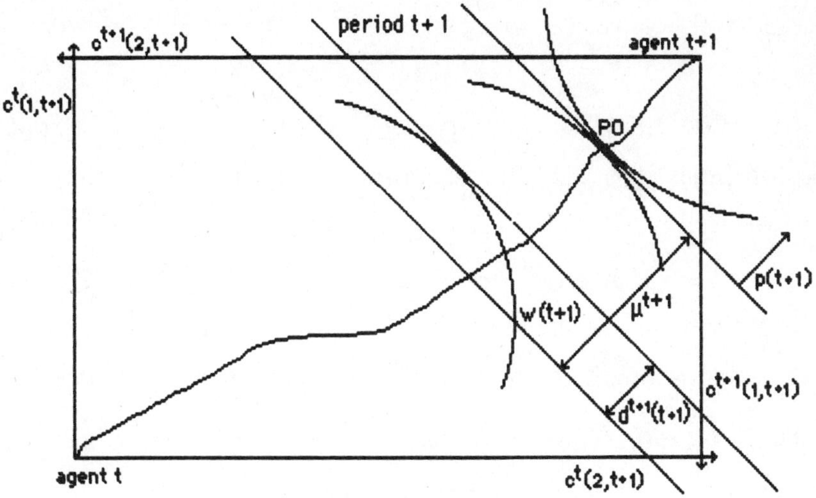

Figure VI.3

From Proposition VI.2 the following Corollaries are straightforward.

Corollary VI.1 Let c be a Pareto optimal walrasian equilibrium consumption allocation. Then, the consumption allocation c belongs to the core.[3]

Proof.- Barter competitive equilibria are associated with M=0. Thus the condition established in Proposition VI.2 is always satisfied. QED.

Corollary VI.2 Let n=1. Then the core of the economy consists only of those Pareto optimal allocations that are walrasian competitive equilibria.[4]

Proof.- For $n=1$ we have that $b^t(t)=b^t(t+1)=0$ for $t=1,2,\ldots$. Thus, accordingly with Proposition VI.2 only competitive equilibria with $M=0$ (i.e. walrasian) can be in the core. QED.

Corollary VI.2 is in fact a restatement of Proposition VI.1 using the Definition VI.5' of sequential individual rationality.

As a matter of fact, Corollary VI.2 could have been presented in a slightly more general way. In view of the proof, this result holds true for n-goods economies in which there exist agents r and s such that $b^r(r)=b^s(s+1)=0$. This case will occur when for some period the endowments allocation w lies on the contract curve.

Corollary VI.2 can be seen also as a limit case when indifference surfaces are flat. It is obvious that for given endowments the value of b depends on the curvature of indifference surfaces. As indifference surfaces become flatter the set of weak Pareto optimum and sequentially individually rational allocations shrinks. At the limit, when indifference surfaces become hiperplanes, the value of b is zero. This situation corresponds to an infinite elasticity of commodity substitution between goods of the same period. Thus, the result for $n=1$ can be seen as a limiting case of an n-good economy in which indifference surfaces become flat. The intuition behind this result is clear. The higher is the level of complementarity between goods the greater the interdependence between generations through the exchange process. Hence, complementarity between goods gives social acceptability of consumption allocations.

VI.5. Core Allocations and Monetary Equilibria

In Corollary VI.1 we have established that all Pareto optimal walrasian equilibria, with $M=0$, belong to the core of the economy and in Corollary VI.2 that for $n=1$ no monetary equilibrium can ever belong to the core. It seems now of interest analysing whether for $n \geq 2$ Pareto optimal monetary equilibria, with $M \neq 0$, can be in the core. In other words, we shall examine whether for many goods economies there exist monetary equilibria satisfying the conditions given in Proposition VI.2.

It does not seem to be possible to establish a general proposition of existence of competitive equilibria in the core. Specifically, we shall examine whether taking the aggregate resources available in each period as given it is possible to redistribute the given endowments among agents of the two coexisting generations in such a way as to grant that some monetary equilibrium belongs to the core.

Let us denote by $\overline{w}(t)$ the aggregate endowments available at period t and by $\overline{w}$ the sequence $\overline{w} = \{\overline{w}(1), \overline{w}(2), \ldots\}$. Since $w \in \mathbf{W}$ it is obvious that $\overline{w} \in \mathbf{W}$ as well. Given a sequence of aggregate endowments $\overline{w}$, we shall denote by $W(\overline{w})$ the set of sequences of individual initial endowments such that

$$w^{t-1}(t)+w^{t}(t)=\overline{w}^{t}, \quad w^{t-s}(t) \in \mathbb{R}^{n}_{+}, \quad s=0,1 \text{ and } t=1,2,\ldots .$$

Let $C(\overline{w})$ be the set of consumption allocations sequences satisfying:

i) $c^{t-1}(t)+c^{t}(t)=\overline{w}^{t}, \quad t=1,2,\ldots$; and

ii) c^{t} is uniformly bounded below by a strictly positive vector y, $y \in \mathbb{R}^{2n}_{++}$, $t=1,2,\ldots$.

Therefore, a consumption allocation sequence c, $c \in C(\bar{w})$, is feasible and belongs to the strict interior of the Edgeworth box for every period t, $t=1,2,\ldots$.

Let us now consider the set $W(\bar{c})$ of all the initial endowments sequences w such that:

i) $w \in W(\bar{w})$; and

ii) $v^{t-1}{}_t(w^{t-1}(t)) \leqq v^{t-1}{}_t(\bar{c}^{t-1}(t))$ and $v^t{}_t(w^t(t)) \leqq v^{t-1}{}_t(\bar{c}^t(t))$, $t=1,2,\ldots$

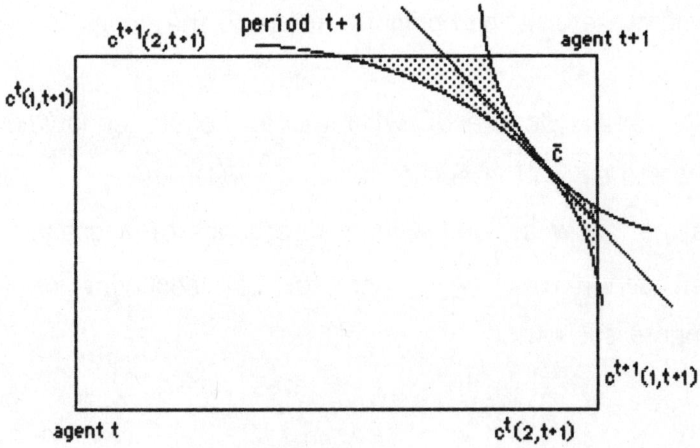

Figure VI.4

Since $\bar{c} \in C(\bar{w})$, by Assumption VI.1 the set $W(\bar{c})$ will have more than one element. This corresponds to the dotted area of Figure VI.4. In fact, this set contains the intersection of the separating hyperplanes and the set of feasible consumption allocations.

Given a Pareto optimal consumption allocation sequence $\bar{c}$, the set $W(\bar{c})$ contains all the initial endowments sequences w for which $\bar{c}$ belongs to the core of the economy. The problem we shall now deal with is whether there exist an endowments allocation sequence $w \in W(\bar{c})$, a strictly positive finite real number M, and a sequence of prices $p \in \mathbf{P}$,such that $\bar{c}$ is a monetary equilibrium accordingly with definition VI.10 and belongs to the core. We shall enquire first about the implementability of consumption allocations as monetary equilibria, to examine later whether they are or not in the core.

Before going into these results we need to define the notion of supporting prices. Moreover, we shall introduce additional assumptions about preferences and the boundedness of individual consumption allocations. This assumption is essential to enable us to use the important proposition by Balasko and Shell [4] in which they provide a complete characterization of Pareto optimal allocations in terms of their supporting price sequences, as defined in Definition VI.11.

Definition VI.11 Let c be a consumption allocation sequence. We shall say that the <u>price sequence</u> $p \in \mathbb{P}$ <u>supports</u> c if and only if, for some suitably chosen endowment sequence $w \in \mathbf{W}$ and finite real number M, $p(t) \cdot c^t(t) + p(t+1) \cdot c^t(t+1) \leqq p(t) \cdot w^t(t) + p(t+1) \cdot w^t(t+1)$ and $u^t(c^t) \geqq u^t(\hat{c}^t)$ for all $\hat{c}^t$ satisfying the budget constraint, for $t=1,2,..$, and for $t=0$ $p(1) \cdot c^0(1) \leqq p(1) \cdot w^0(1) + M$ and $u^0(c^0) \geqq u^0(\hat{c}^0)$ for all $\hat{c}^0$ satisfying the budget constraint.

Balasko and Shell [4] demonstrate that a consumption allocation sequence is weakly Pareto optimal if and only if it has a supporting price sequence.

Assumption VI.3 (a) The Gaussian curvature of consumer (j,t)'s indifference surface through $c^{j,t}$, $0 < c^{j,t} < [c(t), c(t+1)]$ is uniformly bounded from above and from below away from zero;

(b) There exists a constant P, independent of t, such that

$$0 < P \leqq p(i,t)/\|p(t)\|, \quad \text{for } i=1,\ldots,n \text{ and } t=1,2,\ldots .$$

(c) The sequence c is uniformly bounded from above and from below away from zero by a strictly positive vector.

Specifically they show [4, Proposition 5.6.][5] that under Assumptions VI.1 and VI.3 a weakly Pareto optimal consumption allocation sequence c with supporting prices p is Pareto optimal if and only if

$$\text{(VI.4)} \qquad \Sigma 1/\|p(t)\| = +\infty .$$

In view of (VI.4) it is straightforward that

$$\text{(VI.5)} \qquad \text{Lim inf}_{t \to \infty} \|p(t)\| = 0$$

is a sufficient condition for Pareto optimality, as proven by Balasko and Shell [4, Proposition 5.3][6]. As we shall now see, no Pareto optimal consumption allocation with supporting prices satisfying (VI.5) is weakly implementable as a monetary equilibrium.

Definition VI.12 Let $\bar{w} \in \mathbf{W}$ be a sequence of aggregate endowments. The consumption allocation c will be said to be <u>weakly implementable as a monetary equilibrium</u> if there exist a sequence of individual endowments $w \in W(\bar{w})$, a finite real number $M \neq 0$, and a price sequence p such that c can be obtained as a monetary equilibrium, accordingly with Definition VI.10.

Proposition VI.3 Let consumer preferences satisfy Assumptions VI.1, VI.2 and VI.3. A weakly Pareto optimal consumption allocation sequence c is weakly implementable as a monetary equilibrium if and only if its supporting price sequence p satisfies that

$$\operatorname{Lim\,inf}_{t \to \infty} \|p(t)\| \geqq \lambda > 0.$$

<u>Proof</u>.- Consider the weakly Pareto optimal consumption sequence c and the associated sequence of supporting hyperplanes defined by

(VI.6) $$p(t) \cdot c^{t-1}(t) = K(t) \qquad t=1,2,\dots,$$

with $c^t(t) = \bar{w}(t) - c^{t-1}(t)$. This consumption sequence will be weakly implementable as a monetary equilibrium if we can find a sequence of initial endowments $w \in W(\bar{w})$ and $M \neq 0$ such that

$$p(t) \cdot c^{t-1}(t) = p(t) \cdot w^{t-1}(t) + M \ , \quad t=1,2,\dots,$$

that is

(VI.7) $$p(t) \cdot w^{t-1}(t) = K(t) - M \, .$$

Therefore, our problem is to find a value of M for which the sequence of hyperplanes defined by (VI.7) intersects the sequence of feasible endowments allocation, i.e.

$$0 \leqq w^{t-1}(t) \leqq \bar{w}(t) \quad \text{and} \quad w^t(t) = \bar{w}(t) - w^{t-1}(t), \quad t=1,2,\dots \, .$$

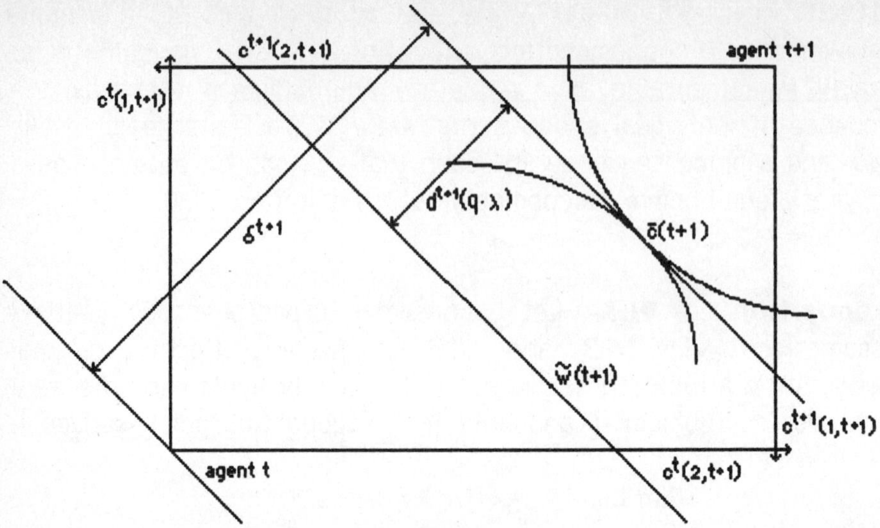

Figure VI.5

Let $d(t,M)$ be the distance between the hyperplanes defined by (VI.6) and (VI.7), that is, $d(t,M) = |M|/\|p(t)\|$, $t=1,2,\ldots$, and $\delta(t)$ the distance between the hyperplanes defined by (VI.6) and the origin, as depicted in Figure VI.5, that is $\delta(t) = K(t)/\|p(t)\|$, $t=1,2,\ldots$.

The necessary and sufficient condition for the sequence of hyperplanes (VI.7) to intersect the set of feasible endowments allocations, and thus c be weakly implementable as a monetary equilibrium is that for some M' , $0<\epsilon\leq |M'| <+\infty$, $d(t,M')<\delta(t)$ and this implies that

$$|M'|<K(t)=\delta(t)\cdot\|p(t)\| \text{ , for } t=1,2,\ldots \text{ .}$$

By assumption VI.3(c) $\delta(t)$ is bounded from above and from below away from 0 , so that there exist q and Q such that

$$0<q\leq \text{Lim inf}_{t\to\infty}\delta(t)\leq \text{Lim sup}_{t\to\infty}\delta(t)\leq Q<+\infty.$$

Thus,

$$q \cdot \text{Lim inf}_{t \to \infty} \|p(t)\| \leqq \text{Lim inf}_{t \to \infty} K(t) \leqq Q \cdot \text{Lim inf}_{t \to \infty} \|p(t)\| \ .$$

If $\text{Lim inf}_{t \to \infty} \|p(t)\| = 0$, there is no $M' \neq 0$ satisfying the necessary and sufficient condition for c be weakly implementable as a monetary equilibrium.

If $\text{Lim inf}_{t \to \infty} \|p(t)\| = \lambda > 0$, for any M' such that $0 < |M'| \leqq q \cdot \lambda$ the sequence of hyperplanes defined by

$$p(t) \cdot w^{t-1}(t) = K(t) - M'$$

intersects the set of feasible endowment allocations. Hence, for any endowment allocation sequence w' in this intersection c can be obtained as a monetary equilibrium supported by the price sequence p and the real number M'. QED.

The intuition of this result[7] is as follows. The consumption allocation c is uniformly bounded above, that is, the amounts consumed are always finite. As we have seen, in a monetary equilibrium the value of money purchases has to remain constant through time. However, when prices converge to zero, the real purchasing power of this constant nominal amount of money tends to infinity. If we were to find an endowments sequence yielding c as a monetary equilibrium, individual initial endowments would have to tend to minus infinity. This would be the only way of keeping demands finite. But, initial endowments have to be non-negative by hypothesis. Thus, it follows that one cannot have monetary equilibria when the supporting prices tend to zero.

Let us finally examine whether monetary equilibria can belong to the core of the economy. In order to give a precise meaning to the discussion of this point we shall introduce the following definition.

Definition VI.13 We shall say that a consumption allocation sequence c is <u>weakly in the core</u> if there exists an initial endowments sequence $w \in W(\bar{w})$ such that c is in the core.

Proposition VI.4 Under Assumptions VI.1, VI.2, and VI.3, and for $n \geq 2$, all Pareto optimal consumption allocation sequences that are weakly implementable as monetary equilibria are also weakly in the core. In other words, let c' be a weakly implementable monetary equilibrium for some $w \in W(\bar{w})$, supporting price sequence p' and M, then there exist a new allocation of endowments $w' \in W(\bar{w})$ and a new M' such that c' belongs to the core and is a monetary equilibrium.

<u>Proof</u> .- Let c' be weakly implementable as a monetary equilibrium, that is, that for all $M \leq q \cdot \lambda$ the intersection of the sequence of hyperplanes $p(t) \cdot w^{t-1}(t) = K(t) - M$, $t=1,2,\ldots$, is non-empty. At the beginning of this section we have shown that the set of endowment allocation sequences for which c' belongs to the core is $W(c')$. Obviously, $W(c') \subset W(\bar{w})$. The point is now whether there exists M', $0 < |M'| \leq q \cdot \lambda$ such that the intersection of the sequence of hyperplanes $p(t) \cdot w^{t-1}(t) = K(t) - M'$ and $W(c')$ is non-empty, as in Figure VI.6. Then for any endowment sequence belonging to this intersection c' would be in the core and could be implemented as a monetary equilibrium with supporting prices p' and monetary purchases M'. We shall work for convenience with $w^t(t) = \bar{w}(t) - w^{t-1}(t)$.

Define the following maximization program

$$\text{Max } p'(t)\cdot w^t(t) \text{ subject to}$$

$$v^t_t(w^t(t)) \leqq v^t_t(c'^t(t)) \text{ and } w \in W(\bar{w}), \text{ for } t=1,2,\ldots \; .$$

Figure VI.6

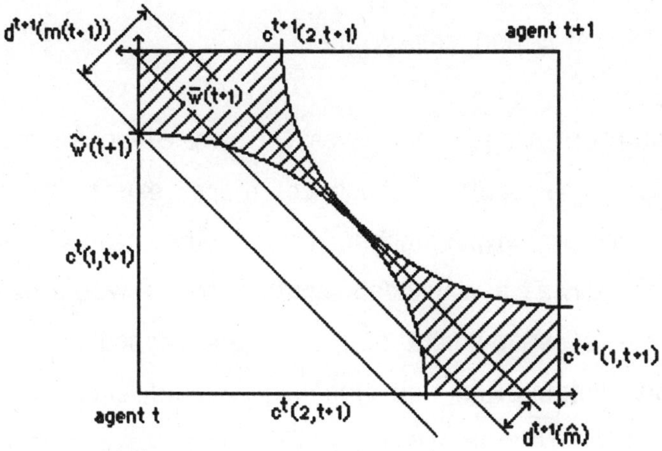

Let $w''^t(t)$, $t=1,2,\ldots$, be the solution to this problem and denote by $M''(t)$

$$M''(t) = \; p'(t)\cdot w''^t(t) - p'(t)\cdot c'^{\,t}(t).$$

Since by Assumption VI.3(c) c' is in the strict interior of $W(\bar{w})$ and preferences are by Assumtion VI.2 strictly quasiconcave,we have that $M''(t)>0$, $t=1,2,\ldots$. Moreover, by Assumption VI.3(a) there exists some $\gamma>0$ such that

$$\text{Lim inf}_{t\to\infty} |M''(t)| \geq \gamma > 0 \ .$$

Therefore, for any M', $0<M'\leqq\gamma$, the intersection of the sequence of hyperplanes

$$p'(t)\cdot w^{\,t}(t) = p'(t)\cdot c'^{\,t}(t) + M'$$

with the set $W(c')$ is non-empty. QED.

The intuition of the proof is as follows. Given a weakly Pareto optimal consumption allocation sequence there exists an associated sequence of supporting hyperplanes. If we were to implement this consumption allocation as a walrasian equilibrium we would need only to choose a sequence of endowment points on the separating hyperplanes, with the additional restriction that this sequence of endowments should satisfy that $w\epsilon W(\bar{w})$. That this is possible is granted by the assumption (VI.3(c)) that consumption allocations are in the strict interior of the Edgeworth boxes corresponding to every period. Note that this endowment allocation would belong to $W(\bar{c})$ too.

When we wish to implement this consumption allocation sequence as a monetary equilibrium, we need chosing endowment points which do not lie on the separating hyperplanes. Specifically, the endowment points have to be on hyperplanes whose distance with respect to the supporting hyperplanes corresponds to the constant nominal purchases of money, M. For every period the geometrical distance between the two hyperplanes is given by $M/\|p(t)\|$. Hence, the point is finding a value of M that given the sequence p generates a sequence of hyperplanes which intersects with the set $W(\bar{c})$. As shown in the proof, for this to be possible it is crucial that the sequence of norms of prices for every period does not converge to zero.

VI.6 Concluding Remarks

In this Chapter we have explored the set of core allocations in an n-good overlapping generations economy and have demonstrated that the set of competitive equilibria is not a subset of the set of core allocations. On the one hand, all Pareto inefficient walrasian equilibria do not belong to the core. On the other hand, competitive monetary equilibria may not belong to the core if the amount of nominal monetary transactions exceeds some bounds.

The fact that walrasian equilibria may not belong to the core of the economy was first demonstrated by Hendricks et al. [36] for the one commodity case. In this respect, the main point is not that the set of walrasian allocations is not a subset of the set of core allocations, but that the intersection between the two sets might be empty. Hendricks et al. [36] attribute this result to the fact that overlapping generations models, to use Shell's [55] words, are characterised by a "double infinity" of agents and commodities. This suggests that the only reason why the standard result for Arrow-Debreu economies does not hold true for overlapping generations models is that the First Fundamental Welfare Theorem does not hold true either. While this is partially true, we shall show in the next Chapter that it is not by any means the whole story. Indeed, we shall demonstrate that with many agents per generation walrasian equilibria may not belong to the core of the economy, in spite of being Pareto optimal.

Besides the theoretical general equilibrium point of view, the results of this Chapter are of some relevance for monetary theory. We have shown that, in one-good economies, monetary equilibria would not belong to the core. As for many goods economies, we demonstrate that there exist bounds limiting the amount of money for a monetary equilibrium to belong to the core. These results are of some interest because one good overlapping generations models have been seen as a satisfactory framework for the analysis of the role of fiat money as a store of value[8]. Generalizations to n-goods models do not seem to provide any significant new insight into the "social contrivance" of fiat money. Yet, this generalization turns out to play a crucial role in preventing all monetary equilibria from being blocked. This is so because intra-period losses faced by individuals heading a blocking coalition might exceed the inter-period benefits. It is remarkable that the social acceptability of fiat money comes from the fact that its acceptance allows for intra-period trade rather than by its virtue of being the sole store of value.

In order to make this point more precise, we can intepret blocking as refusing the existing fiat money carried over by the previous generation. Under this interpretation, our Definition VI.7 of blocking implicitly assumes that money is a means of exchange as well as a store of value. In other words, when refusing fiat money neither intraperiod nor intertemporal trades are possible. Therefore, in this model it is the role of money as a means of exchange, rather than as a store of value, which allows monetary equilibria to be in the core of the economy.

The extent to which the intraperiod losses can refrain agents from blocking monetary allocations obviously depends on the number of individuals every generation is composed of. This case is examined in Chapter VII. As the number of agents of each generation increases, the intra-period losses can be reduced by means of intra-generational exchange and thus refusing money becomes easier. As we shall see, enlarging the economy by replication takes out of the core all monetary equilibria.

In this chapter we have considered monetary equilibria with "outside" money. As a matter of fact, the introduction of "inside" money requires assuming that in each generation there coexist many agents with different preferences. Only in these circumstances we shall have borrowing and lending among agents. This is examined in Chapter VIII. As we shall see the social refusal of money extends to "inside" money. We shall provide an example of a Pareto optimal walrasian equilibrium which does not belong to the core of the economy. In that case, blocking can be interpreted as the sequence of lenders splitting apart to carry out their savings plans with the help of outside money in stead of inside money.

Notes to Chapter VI

1 This result is no longer true for many agents economies as demonstrated in Chapter VII.

2 The essential problem in this kind of model is multiplicity rather than existence, as recently studied by Kehoe and Levine [40], [41], and [42], Geanakoplos and Polemarchakis [30], and Santos [52].

3 This result has been independently demonstrated by Kovenock [43].

4 A similar result is given by Hendricks et al. [36].

5 A similar result was proven by Okuno and Zilcha [47].

6 See also Okuno and Zilcha [47].

7 The fact that consumption allocation sequences with supporting prices converging to zero cannot be monetary equilibria has already been stated, though not rigorously proved, by Hahn [34].

8 See for instance, Kareken and Wallace [39] and Sargent [54]. Grandmont [31] while working with an n-goods overlapping generation model develops most of his arguments and demonstrations for one good.

Chapter VII Competitive Equilibria and the Core. Many agents per generation

VII.1. Introduction

Overlapping generations models have been recently analysed from a game theoretical point of view. Specifically, the core of economies with an overlapping generations structure has been studied by Hendricks et al. [36], Kovenock [43], and Chae [16]. Related concepts such as bounded core and short-run core have been dealt with by Hendricks et al. [36] and Chae [16], Chae and Esteban [17]. In this Chapter we shall examine the relation between competitive equilibria and the core in overlapping generations economies with many agents per generation.

For finite horizon Arrow-Debreu economies the relations between efficiency, competitive equilibria and core have been established in a series of well-know theorems, as in Arrow and Hahn [1] for instance. On the one hand, the Fundamental Welfare Theorems state that competitive equilibria are Pareto optimal and that Pareto optimal allocations are implementable as competitive equilibria. On the other hand, we have the result that every consumption allocation implementable as a competitive equilibrium belongs to the core of the economy for all the endowments allocations for which it can be obtained as a competitive equilibrium.

Samuelson [50] himself made it plain that the Fundamental Welfare Theorems were not valid in overlapping generations economies. However, in an important paper Balasko and Shell [4] have demonstrated that an equivalence between competitive and efficient allocations can be obtained by an appropriate redefinition of efficiency. They introduce the notion of weak Pareto optimality and demonstrate that it is satisfied by every competitive equilibrium. Likewise, Chae's [16] work can be seen as an attempt at saving the relation between competitive equilibria and core by redefining the notion of socially viable allocations. He proposes the use of the concept of the bounded core and shows that the competitive equilibria of the economy belong to the bounded core.

In this chapter we examine the relation between the notions of Pareto optimality, competitive equilibria and core. At variance with the works reported above, our approach does not consist in redefining the concepts of dynamic efficiency and/or core. Instead, we shall establish the relations between the standard concepts but restricted to the "classical set". The classical set, **C**, consists of those competitive equilibrium allocations which cannot be affected by monetary tax-tranfers policies, as studied by Balasko and Shell [5] and [7]. Specifically our results are the following: i) the classical set is a subset of the set of Pareto optimal allocations; and ii) every competitive equilibrium in the classical set belongs to the core. The fact that competitive equilibria not in the classical set may not be Pareto optimal or not belong to the core suggests that the fundamental singularity of overlapping generations models lies in the possibility of competitive equilibria in which in every period there are consumers who violate their budget constraint in that period.

Let us now briefly discuss the relation between these results, the existing literature and the results obtained in the previous Chapter. For the case of exchange economies with one agent per generation, Hendricks et al. [36] and our Chapter VI have demonstrated that all Pareto optimal walrasian equilibria belong to the core. We know that in overlapping generations economies walrasian equilibria might not be

Pareto optimal and thus cannot belong to the core. It can be tempting to conclude, as suggested by Hendricks et al. [36], that the only reason why walrasian equilibria may not belong to the core is that they may fail to be dynamically efficient. That this is not the case for economies with many agents per generation has been made plain by Kovenock [43] who has provided an example of a Pareto optimal walrasian equilibrium which does not belong to the core and the core is empty. In this respect, we give here another example of a Pareto optimal walrasian allocation which does not belong to the core, while the core is not empty. Our example is instructive from another point of view. It shows that consumption allocations corresponding to equilibria with inside money might be blocked by the coalition formed by the sequence of lenders. They can grant for themselves a consumption allocation which could be interpreted as a subeconomy that substitutes fiat money for inside money. Further, we show that these examples are by no means pathological. We demonstrate in Proposition VII.4 that for all competitive consumption allocations with price sequence such that $\text{Lim inf}_{t \to \infty} \|p(t)\| \geqq \epsilon > 0$ one can construct distributions of initial endowments for which that equilibrium consumption allocation is not in the core. Moreover, we prove in Proposition VII.3 that $\text{Lim inf}_{t \to \infty} \|p(t)\| = 0$ is a sufficient condition for a competitive equilibrium to belong to the core of the economy, irrespective of the distribution of endowments. This result is stronger than Chae's [16] Theorem 4.1, where with a continuum of agents he finds that a sufficient condition for an allocation to belong to the core is that the present value of the total endowment be finite.

Besides the eventual interest of these results for general equilibrium theory, the propositions presented in this Chapter have a special bearing on monetary theory. Specifically, monetary and IOU equilibria can never satisfy the sufficiency condition on prices for a competitive equilibrium to belong to the core. Moreover, by Proposition VII.4, we can always find examples of Pareto optimal monetary and/or IOU equilibria not belonging to the core of the economy. We devote one section of this Chapter to the analysis of the specific problems posed by the relation between monetary equilibria and the core. There we show that every monetary equilibrium becomes excluded from the core upon replication of the economy.

All these results are rather negative concerning the suitability of overlapping generations models for the analysis of fiat money. In our discussion at the end of the Chapter we suggest that our results can be interpreted as a formal demonstration of Clower's [19] observation that, as quoted in de Vries[58], «money differs from other commodities in being universally acceptable as an exchange intermediary by virtue not of individual choice but rather by virtue of social contrivance» (pp.14-15).

The Chapter is structured as follows. Section 2 contains the definitions and assumptions. In section 3 we define and characterize the classical set. Section 4 provides an example of a walrasian Pareto optimal equilibrium which does not belong to the core, while the core is non empty. The relation between efficiency, competitive equilibria and the core of the economy is the object of section 5. There we state our main propositions. Section 6 focusses on monetary equilibria and we prove that monetary equilibria do not belong to the core of large economies. The Chapter ends with a discussion of the implications of our propositions for monetary theory. We examine the relation with the work of Douglas Gale [18] on the trustworthiness of intertemporal allocations and the role of money. We argue that our results provide a rationale for the lack of trust on the IOU competitive equilibria.

VII.2.- Notation, Assumptions and Definitions

We shall assume a pure exchange economy with n perishable commodities available at every date. In every period t, t=1,2,..., a number m of agents is born[1] and live for two periods. At the beginning of this economy there exists a generation previously born at time $t=0$. Let $c^{j,t}(i,t+s)$ be the consumption of good i $(i=1,2,\ldots,n)$ at period $t+s$ $(s=0,1)$ $(t=1,2,\ldots)$ by consumer j $(j=1,2,\ldots,m)$ born at t $(t=0,1,2,\ldots)$, $c^{j,t}(t+s)\in\mathbb{R}^n_+$ be the consumption vector at period $t+s$ $(s=0,1)$ by agent j born at t, $c^{j,t}\in\mathbb{R}^{2n}_+$ the vector of consumptions corresponding to the two periods that agent will be alive, $c^t(t+s)\in\mathbb{R}^n_+$ be the vector of consumption by generation t at period $t+s$, and $c^t\in\mathbb{R}^{2n}_+$ the vector of consumptions of generation t. For generation $t=0$ we have that $c^0=c^0(1)$ and, of course, $c^0\in\mathbb{R}^n_+$. We shall use c to denote the sequence $c=\{c^0,c^1,c^2,\ldots\}$. Similarly, we shall denote by $w^{j,t}(i,t+s)$ the endowment of good i at $t+s$ by agent j born at period t, $w^{j,t}(t+s)\in\mathbb{R}^n_+$ be the endowment vector at period $t+s$ $(s=0,1)$ of agent j born at t, $w^{j,t}\in\mathbb{R}^{2n}_+$ the vector of endowments corresponding to the two periods that agent will be alive, $w^t(t+s)\in\mathbb{R}^n_+$ be the vector of endowments of generation t at period $t+s$, and $w^t\in\mathbb{R}^{2n}_+$ the vector of endowments of generation t. Again, for generation $t=0$ we have that $w^0=w^0(1)$ and, of course, $w^0\in\mathbb{R}^n_+$. Finally, we shall denote by w the sequence $w=\{w^0,w^1,w^2,\ldots\}$. Let $\mathbf{W}$ be the set of all sequences w which are uniformly bounded from above.

Let us denote by $\overline{w}(t)$ the aggregate endowments available at period t and by $\overline{w}$ the sequence $\overline{w} = \{\overline{w}(1), \overline{w}(2), \dots\}$. Since $w \in \mathbf{W}$ it is obvious that $\overline{w} \in \mathbf{W}$ as well. Given a sequence of aggregate endowments $\overline{w}$, we shall denote by $W(\overline{w})$ the set of sequences of individual initial endowments such that

$$w^{t-1}(t) + w^{t}(t) = \overline{w}^{t}, \quad w^{t-s}(t) \in \mathbb{R}^{n}_{+}, \; s=0,1 \text{ and } t=1,2,\dots .$$

Preferences of consumer j born at t can be represented by a utility function $u^{j,t}: \mathbb{R}^{2n}_{+} \to \mathbb{R}$, for $t=1,2,\dots$ and $u^{j,0}: \mathbb{R}^{n}_{+} \to \mathbb{R}$, for $t=0$, and $j=1,\dots,m$.

Assumption VII.1 $u^{j,t}$ has strictly positive first order partial derivatives and is strictly quasi-concave.

Definition VII.1 A consumption allocation sequence c is <u>feasible</u> if

$$c^{t-1}(t) + c^{t}(t) = c(t) \leqq w^{t-1}(t) + w^{t}(t) = w(t) \qquad \text{for } t=1,2,\dots .$$

Definition VII.2 The feasible consumption allocation sequence c is <u>Pareto optimal</u> if there is no $\hat{c}$ such that : i) $\hat{c}$ is feasible; and ii) $u^{j,t}(\hat{c}^{j,t}) \geqq u^{j,t}(c^{j,t})$ for $t=0,1,2,\dots$, and $j=1,\dots,m$ with at least one strict inequality.

Definition VII.3 The feasible consumption allocation sequence c is <u>weakly Pareto optimal</u> if there is no $\hat{c}$ such that : i) $\hat{c}$ is feasible; ii) $\hat{c}^{j,t} = c^{j,t}$ except for a finite number of periods ; and iii) $u^{j,t}(\hat{c}^{j,t}) \geqq u^{j,t}(c^{j,t})$ for $t=0,1,2,\dots$, and $j=1,\dots m$,with at least one strict inequality.

Full information and perfect foresight is assumed throughout the Chapter. Let $p(i,t)$ denote the price of commodity i delivered at period t, $i=1,\ldots,n$ and $t=1,2,\ldots$, $p(t)$ the vector $(p(1,t),\ldots,p(n,t))\in\mathbb{R}^n_+$, and p the price sequence $p=\{p(1),p(2),\ldots\}$. We shall normalize by setting $p(1,1)=1$ and we shall denote by **P** the set of such price sequences, i.e. $\mathbf{P}=\{p/p(1,1)=1, p(t)\in\mathbb{R}^n_+\}$.

Definition VII.4 Let c be a consumption allocation sequence. We shall say that the <u>price sequence</u> $p\in\mathbb{P}$ <u>supports</u> c if and only if, for some suitably chosen endowment sequence $w\in\mathbf{W}$, we have that

$$p(t)\cdot c^{j,t}(t) + p(t+1)\cdot c^{j,t}(t+1) \leqq p(t)\cdot w^{j,t}(t) + p(t+1)\cdot w^{j,t}(t+1)$$

and $u^{j,t}(c^{j,t})\geqq u^{j,t}(\hat{c}^{j,t})$ for all $\hat{c}^{j,t}$ satisfying the budget constraint, for $j=1,\ldots,m$ and $t=1,2,\ldots$, and for $t=0$

$$p(1)\cdot c^{j,0}(1)\leqq p(1)\cdot w^{j,0}(1)$$

and $u^{j,0}(c^{j,0})\geqq u^{j,0}(\hat{c}^{j,0})$ for all $\hat{c}^{j,0}$ satisfying the budget constraint, $j=1,\ldots m$.

Further, for the sequence $y=\{y^0,y^1,y^2,\ldots\}$, with $y^t\in\mathbb{R}^m_+$, we shall say that (p,y) is a <u>price-income equilibrium</u> if

$$p(t)\cdot c^{j,t}(t) + p(t+1)\cdot c^{j,t}(t+1) = y^{j,t}, \quad j=1,\ldots,m \text{ and } t=1,2,\ldots ,$$

and

$$p(1)\cdot c^{j,0}(1) = y^{j,0}, \quad j=1,\ldots,m .$$

Throughout the Chapter we shall make extensive use of Balasko and Shell's [4] characterization of Pareto optimum allocations.[2] Therefore, we shall assume that the conditions given in their Theorem 5.3 are satisfied.

Assumption VII.2 (a) The Gaussian curvature of consumer (j,t)'s indifference surface through $c^{j,t}$, $0<c^{j,t}<[c(t),c(t+1)]$ is uniformly bounded from above and from below away from zero;

(b) There exists a constant P, independent of t, such that

$$0 < P \leqq p(i,t)/\|p(t)\|, \quad \text{for } i=1,\dots,n \text{ and } t=1,2,\dots .$$

(c) The sequence c is uniformly bounded from above and from below away from zero by a strictly positive vector.

We shall borrow from Chapter V the definitions of coalition and core of the economy and adapt them to the case of many consumers per generation.

Definition VII.5 A coalition is a non-empty connected subset S of the set of all agents.

We shall denote by S_t the set of all agents born at period t which belong to coalition S, so that, $S_t \subseteq S$. Then, by the connectedness of S we mean that if $S_t \neq \emptyset$ and $S_{t+k} \neq \emptyset$, then $S_{t+r} \neq \emptyset$, $r=1,\dots,k-1$.

A coalition will thus be formed by a chain of generations, which might not include all their members. We shall denote by f the first of such generations, i.e. $f = \min\{t / S_t \neq \emptyset\}$.

Definition VII.6 An allocation $\bar{c}$ is blocked by coalition S if there exists another allocation c such that:

i) c is feasible for coalition S, i.e.

$$\sum_{j \in S_{t-1}} c^{j,t-1}(t) + \sum_{j \in S_t} c^{j,t}(t) = \sum_{j \in S_{t-1}} w^{j,t-1}(t) + \sum_{j \in S_t} w^{j,t}(t), \text{ for all } S_t \in S,$$ [3]

ii) $u^{j,t}(c^{j,t}) \geqq u^{j,t}(\bar{c}^{j,t})$ for all agents $(j,t) \in S$, with at least one strict inequality for some agent $(j,t) \in S_t$.

Definition VII.7 The core of an economy is the set of all allocations that are feasible and not blocked by any coalition.

VII.3. The Classical Set: Definition and Characterization

We shall now formally define and characterize the classical set. In order to do so we shall make use of the notion of consistency as introduced in Balasko and Shell [5] and [7].

Definition VII.8 We shall say that the endowments allocation sequence $w \in \mathbf{W}$ is consistent with the price-income equilibrium (p,y) associated with the consumption allocation sequence c if :
$p(t)\cdot c^{j,t}(t)+p(t+1)\cdot c^{j,t}(t+1) = p(t)\cdot w^{j,t}(t) \ \ p(t+1)\cdot w^{j,t}(t+1) = y^{j,t}$,
for $j=1,\dots m$ and $t=0,1,2,\dots$.

We shall denote by $\mathbf{W}(c)$ the set of sequences w consistent with the price-income equilibrium associated with c. Let us now introduce the notion of sequential consistency in which the single condition of lifetime income consistency is replaced by a sequence of consistency conditions, one for every period. More precisely, we require this condition be satisfied in the long-run.

Let us denote by $b^{j,t}(t)=\max\{ p(t)\cdot[c^{j,t}(t)-w^{j,t}(t)],0\}$, $j=1,\dots m$,

and by $b^t(t)$ and $B^t(t)$,

$$b^t(t)=\Sigma b^{j,t}(t) \text{ and } B^t(t)=\max\{b^{1,t},\dots,b^{j,t},\dots b^{m,t}\}\ ,\ t=1,2,\dots .$$

Definition VII.9 We shall say that the endowments allocation sequence $w \in \mathbf{W}$ is sequentially consistent with the price-income equilibrium (p,y) associated with the consumption allocation sequence c if $w \in \mathbf{W}(c)$ and $\liminf_{t\to\infty} B^t(t)=0$.

We shall denote by $\mathbf{W}^s(c)$ the set of endowment allocations w sequentially consistent with the price-income equilibrium associated with c. Obviously $\mathbf{W}^s(c) \subseteq \mathbf{W}(c)$. As we shall see, there are consumption allocations such that $\mathbf{W}^s(c)=\mathbf{W}(c)$, that is, that can only be implemented as equilibria with the property that in the long-run every agent balances his budget constraint in every period of his life. Following Balasko and Shell [5] and [7], we can interpret this property as implying that the government cannot alter the equilibrium allocation by means of monetary taxes and/or transfers, i.e. there are no *bona fide* monetary policies. It is in this sense that we borrow from David Gale [27] the word <u>classical</u> to denote the set of equilibrium allocations in which there is no room for monetary policies. In other words, allocations in the classical set cannot be a competitive equilibrium with either inside or outside money.

We are now in a position to define the classical set.

Definition VII.10 We shall say that the consumption allocation sequence c belongs to the classical set, $c \in \mathbf{C}$, if and only if $\mathbf{W}^s(c)=\mathbf{W}(c)$, i.e. all $w \in \mathbf{W}(c)$ are sequentially consistent with the corresponding price-income equilibrium (p,y).

The following Proposition provides a characterization of the consumption allocation sequences in the classical set by means of their supporting prices.

Proposition VII.1 Let Assumptions VII.1 and VII.2 be satisfied. The consumption allocation sequence c belongs to the classical set if and only if its sequence of supporting prices satisfies that

$$\operatorname{Lim\,inf}_{t \to \infty} \|p(t)\| = 0 .$$

<u>Proof</u>.- Let us start by showing that $\operatorname{Lim\,inf}_{t \to \infty} \|p(t)\| = 0$

implies that $\text{Lim inf}_{t\to\infty} B^t(t)=0$.

Let us denote by the superscript k the agent with the highest amount of borrowing in each generation, i.e.

$$B^t(t)= p(t)\cdot[c^{k,t}(t)-w^{k,t}(t)].$$

It is obvious that

$$\|p(t)\|\cdot\|c^{k,t}(t)-w^{k,t}(t)\|\geqq p(t)\cdot[c^{k,t}(t)-w^{k,t}(t)]=B^t(t).$$

By Assumption VII.2(c) the value of $\|c^{k,t}(t)-w^{k,t}(t)\|$ is uniformly bounded above by some $K<+\infty$. Thus we can write the following inequalities

$$\|p(t)\|\cdot K \geqq \|p(t)\|\cdot\|c^{k,t}(t)-w^{k,t}(t)\| \geqq p(t)\cdot[c^{k,t}(t)-w^{k,t}(t)]=B^t(t)\geqq 0.$$

Therefore when $\text{Lim inf}_{t\to\infty}\|p(t)\| = 0$ it must be that $\text{Lim inf}_{t\to\infty} B^t(t) = 0$. This proves necessity.

For sufficiency one can just follow the same steps as in Proposition VI.3. Consider for instance the endowments allocation sequence w and the sequence of real numbers $b=\{b^1,b^2,\dots\}$, $b(t)\in\mathbb{R}$ such that $w^{j,t}=c^{j,t}$ $j=3,4,\dots,m$ and $t=0,1,2,\dots$ and $w^{1,t}$ and $w^{2,t}$ satisfying

$$p(t)[c^{1,t}(t)-w^{1,t}(t)]=b^t=-p(t)[c^{2,t}(t)-w^{2,t}(t)]=$$
$$=-p(t+1)[c^{1,t}(t+1)-w^{1,t}(t+1)]=p(t+1)[c^{2,t}(t+1)-w^{2,t}(t+1)].$$

Observe that $b^t = B^t(t)$. By Proposition VI.3 the sequence b

exists and is uniformly bounded below by $\beta>0$. Further, the endowments allocation sequence thus constructed is such that $w\in\mathbf{W}(c)$ and hence c is a competitive equilibrium. QED.

As we have already pointed out, whereas in finite horizon Arrow-Debreu economies the classical set coincides with the set of Pareto optimal allocations, in overlapping generations economies this is not so. We know from the paper by Balasko and Shell [4] that all the consumption allocations with supporting prices p satisfying that $\sum 1/\|p(t)\|=+\infty$ are Pareto optimal. Thus there certainly exist Pareto optimal allocations which do not belong to the classical set.

VII.4 Competitive Equilibria and the Core : an example

We shall start by giving an example of an economy in which a Pareto optimal non-monetary competitive equilibrium does not belong to the core of the economy, while the set of core allocations is non-empty.[4]

Consider a one-good economy with two agents a and b per period with identical preferences $u=[c^t(t)c^t(t+1)]^{1/2}$ for $t=1,2,\ldots$ and $u=[c^0(1)]^{1/2}$ for agents of generation $t=0$. Agents have endowments $w^{a,t}=(1.5,0.5)$ and $w^{b,t}=(0.5,1.5)$ for $t=1,2,\ldots$ and $w^{a,0}=0.5$ and $w^{b,0}=1.5$ for $t=0$.

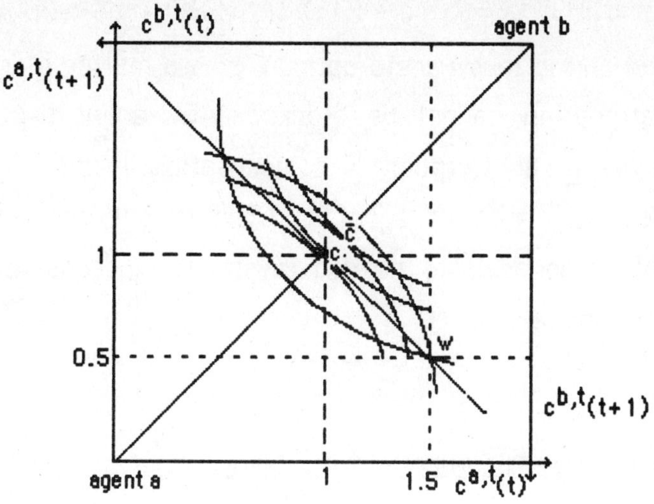

Figure VII.1

The consumption allocation $c^{a,t}(t) = c^{a,t}(t+1) = c^{b,t}(t) = c^{b,t}(t+1) = 1$ is a walrasian equilibrium with equilibrium price sequence $p(t)=1$, for $t=1,2,\dots$, and $c^{a,0}(1)=0.5$ and $c^{b,0}(1)=1.5$. This walrasian allocation is Pareto optimal because the sum of the inverse of prices diverges, thus satisfying Balasko and Shell's criterion. This allocation however does not belong to the core because it would be blocked by the coalition formed by agents (a,t) $t=1,2,\dots$ with consumption allocation $\tilde{c}^{a,1}(1.5,1)$ and $\tilde{c}^{a,t}=(1,1)$ for $t=2,3,\dots$. Note that the original consumption allocation is a walrasian equilibrium with inside money with agents of type "a" behaving as lenders and those of type "b" as borrowers. The blocking coalition is formed by the sequence of lenders who find preferable substituting outside money for inside money.

The set of core allocations is not empty. Consider for instance the weakly Pareto optimal allocation $\bar{c}^{a,0}(1)=0.5$ and $\bar{c}^{b,0}(1)=1.5$,

$\bar{c}^{a,t}=(1.1,1.1)$ and $\bar{c}^{b,t}=(0.9,0.9)$, $t=1,2,\ldots$. This allocation has supporting prices $p(t)=1$ and is thus Pareto optimal. It is a matter of routine to check that this allocation cannot be blocked. Any agent heading a blocking coalition needs a strictly positive compensation in the subsequent period . But no matter the type of agent he tries to get into the coalition, the sequence of compensations needed is strictly increasing and eventually becomes unfeasible.

VII.5 Competitive Equilibria with Many Agents: Walrasian, IOU and Monetary

It is obvious that whereas with one agent per generation we could have two types of competitive equilibria, namely walrasian and monetary, with many agents, the possibility of borrowing and lending between agents of the same generation allows for a new type of competitive equilibrium. We shall call IOU the competitive equilibria in which while fiat,outside money is not used agents engage in trades involving borrowing and lending. Let us now introduce the formal definitions.

Definition VII.11 A competitive equilibrium is a sequence of commodity prices p, real number M and vector $\mu=(\mu^1,\ldots\mu^m)$, $\mu\in\mathbb{R}^m$, $\sum_j|\mu^j|=|\sum_j\mu^j|=|M|$, an endowments allocation sequence $w\in\mathbf{W}$, and a consumption allocation sequence c such that:

i) $p(t)\cdot c^{j,t}(t)+p(t+1)\cdot c^{j,t}(t+1)\leqq p(t)\cdot w^{j,t}(t)+p(t+1)\cdot w^{j,t}(t+1)$ and $u^{j,t}(c^{j,t})\geqq u^{j,t}(\hat{c}^{j,t})$ for all $\hat{c}^t$ satisfying the budget constraint, for $t=1,2,\ldots$ and $j=1,\ldots,m$, and for $t=0$ $p(1)\cdot c^{j,0}(1)\leqq p(1)\cdot w^{j,0}(1)+\mu^j$ and $u^{j,0}(c^{j,0})\geqq u^{j,0}(\hat{c}^{j,0})$ for all $\hat{c}^{j,0}$ satisfying the budget constraint; and

ii) $c^{t-1}(t) + c^t(t) = w^{t-1}(t) + w^t(t)$ for $t=1,2,...$.

We shall call monetary equilibria those competitive equilibria such that $p(t+1)\cdot(c^t(t+1)-w^t(t+1))=M$, $t=0,1,2,...$ for some $M\neq 0$. The competitive equilibria with $M=0$ can be either IOU or walrasian equilibria. There being many agents per generation, we may have that $p(t+1)\cdot(c^{j,t}(t+1)-w^{j,t}(t+1))\neq 0$ for some j, while $M=0$ for the generation as an aggregate. Indeed agents may not balance their budgets in every period if there is borrowing and lending between agents of the same generation. Further, along the sequence we can have generations in which every agent balances his budget constraint in every period of his life, followed by generations in which there is active borrowing and lending between individuals of the same generation. Therefore, whilst in monetary equilibria fiat money is necessarily purchased in every period along the full sequence, in non-monetary equilibria IOUs may only be used in some periods. Since the possibility of analysing the long run behaviour of allocations is inherent to overlapping generations economies, we shall call those competitive equilibria in which IOUs are used in the long run IOU equilibria .

In order to make this notion precise, let us define $b^{j,t}(t)$ as,

$$b^{j,t}(t) = \max\{p(t)\cdot[c^{j,t}(t)-w^{j,t}(t)],0\}, \quad j=1,...,m \quad \text{and} \quad t=1,2,... ,$$

and $b^t(t)$ and $B^t(t)$ as

$$b^t(t) = \sum_j b^{j,t}(t) \quad \text{and} \quad B^t(t) = \max\{b^{1,t}(t),...,b^{j,t}(t),...,b^{m,t}(t)\}.$$

The value $b^{j,t}(t)$ will denote the amount of borrowing engaged by each individual borrower of the economy, $b^t(t)$ the aggregate amount of internal borrowing/lending underwritten by generation t and $B^t(t)$ the maximum amount of individual borrowing in generation t at period t .

Definition VII.12 Let $w \in \mathbf{W}$ and let c be a competitive equilibrium consumption allocation sequence with equilibrium prices $p \in \mathbf{P}$ and $M=0$. We shall say that this competitive equilibrium is an <u>IOU equilibrium</u> when $\text{Lim inf}_{t\to\infty} b^t(t) \geq \beta > 0$ and a <u>walrasian equilibrium</u> otherwise.

Thus, in IOU equilibria there exists a date beyond which a strictly positive amount of IOUs is issued by every generation.

It is quite obvious that any autarkic Pareto optimal competitive equilibrium, i.e. one in which $c^{j,t} = w^{j,t}$ $j=1,\ldots,m$ and $t=1,2,\ldots,$ will belong to the core of the economy. We shall study the relationship between non-autarkic competitive equilibria and the core.

Proposition VII.2 Let Assumption VII.1 be satisfied. Let c be a consumption allocation sequence and p its supporting price sequence. Then if $\text{Lim inf}_{t\to\infty} \|p(t)\| = 0$ the consumption allocation c belongs to the core for every consistent endowments sequence $w \in \mathbf{W}(c)$.[5]

<u>Proof</u>.- First notice that a price sequence with $\text{Lim inf}_{t\to\infty} \|p(t)\| = 0$ cannot correspond to a monetary equilibrium as shown, for instance, in Chapter VI.

Let us assume that c is blocked by coalition S with consumption allocation $\tilde{c}$. Without loss of generality we shall assume that $u^{j,t}(\tilde{c}^{j,t}) > u^{j,t}(c^{j,t})$ for some $(j,f) \in S_f$.

For any agent $(j,t)\epsilon S_t$, $\tilde{c}^{j,t}$ must not be dispreferred to $c^{j,t}$, so that,

$$\text{(VII.1)} \qquad p(t)\cdot[\tilde{c}^{j,t}(t)-c^{j,t}(t)]+p(t+1)\cdot[\tilde{c}^{j,t}(t+1)-c^{j,t}(t+1)]\geqq 0,$$

for all $(j,t)\epsilon S$.

Since by assumption $\tilde{c}$ is strictly prefered to c by some member of generation f, we have that condition (VII.1) holds as a strict inequality for some agent $(j,f)\epsilon S_f$. From the individual budget constraints we have that

$$p(t)\cdot c^{j,t}(t)+p(t+1)\cdot c^{j,t}(t+1) = p(t)\cdot w^{j,t}(t)+p(t+1)\cdot w^{j,t}(t+1)$$

for all (j,t).

Substituting in (VII.1) we obtain

$$\text{(VII.2)} \quad p(t)\cdot[\tilde{c}^{j,t}(t)-w^{j,t}(t)]+p(t+1)\cdot[\tilde{c}^{j,t}(t+1)-w^{j,t}(t+1)]\geqq 0,$$

for all $(j,t)\epsilon S$, with strict inequality for some $(j,f)\epsilon S_f$.

Adding over all $(j,t)\epsilon S_t$, we have

$$\text{(VII.3)} \qquad p(t)\cdot\sum_{j\epsilon S_t}[\tilde{c}^{j,t}(t)-w^{j,t}(t)]+p(t+1)\cdot\sum_{j\epsilon S_t}[\tilde{c}^{j,t}(t+1)-w^{j,t}(t+1)]\geqq 0$$

for $t \geqq f$, with strict inequality for $t=f$.

Consumption allocation $\tilde{c}$ must be feasible for the coalition members, that is,

$$\text{(VII.4)} \qquad \sum_{j\epsilon S_{t-1}}[\tilde{c}^{j,t-1}(t)-w^{j,t-1}(t)]+\sum_{j\epsilon S_t}[\tilde{c}^{j,t}(t)-w^{j,t}(t)]= 0 \text{ for } t\geqq f.$$

Combining (VII.3) and (VII.4) we obtain

$$p(t+1)\cdot\sum_{j\in S_t}[\tilde{c}^{j,t}(t+1)-w^{j,t}(t+1)]\geqq p(t)\cdot\sum_{j\in S_{t-1}}[\tilde{c}^{j,t-1}(t)-w^{j,t-1}(t)]\geqq\ldots\geqq$$

(VII.5)

$$\geqq p(f+1)\cdot\sum_{j\in S_f}[\tilde{c}^{j,f}(f+1)-w^{j,f}(f+1)] \quad , \text{ for } \quad t\geqq f+1.$$

We shall now show that

$$p(f+1)\cdot\sum_{j\in S_f}[\tilde{c}^{j,f}(f+1)-w^{j,f}(f+1)]>0.$$

If $f=0$, this follows from the fact that $\tilde{c}^{j,0}(1)$ must be strictly preferred to $c^{j,0}(1)$ for some $(j,0)\epsilon S_0$. If $f>0$ the feasibility condition (VII.4) requires that

$$\sum_{j\in S_f}[\tilde{c}^{j,f}(f)-w^{j,f}(f)] =0.$$

Thus, from (VII.3) and bearing in mind that $\tilde{c}^{j,f}$ must be strictly preferred to $c^{j,f}$, it follows the above inequality.

The terms of the sequence of inequalities in (VII.5) can be bounded above by

$$\|p(t+1)\|\cdot\|\sum_{j\in S_t}[\tilde{c}^{j,t}(t+1)-w^{j,t}(t+1)]\|\geqq p(t+1)\cdot\sum_{j\in S_t}[\tilde{c}^{j,t}(t+1)-w^{j,t}(t+1)].$$

For economies with $w\epsilon\mathbf{W}$

$$\|\sum_{j\in S_t}[\tilde{c}^{j,t}(t+1)-w^{j,t}(t+1)]\| \text{ is uniformly bounded above.}$$

Hence, if $\text{Lim inf}_{t\to\infty}\|p(t)\| = 0$ it must be that

$$\text{Lim inf}_{t\to\infty}\, p(t+1)\cdot\sum_{j\in S_t}[\tilde{c}^{j,t}(t+1)-w^{j,t}(t+1)]=0.$$

Therefore, there does not exist a sequence $\tilde{c}$ satisfying (VII.1) and (VII.4) and c cannot be blocked. QED.

We shall now study the circumstances under which a competitive equilibrium would not belong to the core of the economy.

Proposition VII.3 Let Assumptions VII.1 and VII.2 be satisfied and let $w \in \mathbf{W}$. Let c be a competitive equilibrium consumption allocation and p the equilibrium price sequence with Lim $\inf_{t \to \infty} \|p(t)\| \geq \epsilon > 0$. Then there exists a distribution $w' \in \mathbf{W(c)}$ for which c is a competitive equilibrium with the same prices p and does not belong to the core.

Proof.- Let us start by pointing out that for any endowments sequence $w \in \mathbf{W}$ such that

(VII.6) $\quad w^t(t) = c^t(t)$ and $w^t(t+1) = c^t(t+1)$, $t=0,1,2,\ldots,$ and

(VII.7) $\quad p(t)\cdot[c^{j,t}(t)-w^{j,t}(t)]+p(t+1)\cdot[c^{j,t}(t+1)-w^{j,t}(t+1)]=0,$

$j=1,\ldots,m$ and $t=0,1,2,\ldots$,

the consumption allocation c will be a competitive equilibrium.

In order to prove the proposition we need to provide an example of reallocation of initial endowments for which the equilibrium consumption allocation under consideration does not belong to the core. We shall consider in the first place the one-commodity case, i.e. n=1. Moreover, we shall restrict to reallocations of endowments such that $w^{j,t} = c^{j,t}$ for $j=3,4,\ldots,m$ and $t=1,2,\ldots$, so that the problem is reduced to finding an appropriate distribution of endowments among two agents in each generation, agents 1 and 2.

A clear case of endowment allocation for which c is not in the core is the one satisfying

$$\text{(VII.8)} \qquad 0 < c^{1,t}(t+1) - w^{1,t}(t+1) \leqq w^{1,t+1}(t+1), \qquad t=1,2,\ldots$$

In that case the coalition formed by the sequence of agents (1,t), t=1,2,... would block c .

We need now to show that there exists an endowments allocations sequence satisfying (VII.8) as well as (VII.6) and (VII.7). Using (VII.7), (VII.8) can be rewritten as

$$\text{(VII.9)} \qquad 0<c^{1,t}(t+1)-w^{1,t}(t+1)\leqq$$

$$\leqq (p^{t+2}/p^{t+1})(c^{1,t+1}(t+2)-w^{1,t+1}(t+2).$$

Let us construct the endowment sequence w satisfying (VII.9) such that

$$\text{(VII.10)} \qquad w^{j,t}(t+1)=c^{j,t}(t+1) - [w^{1,1}(1)-c^{1,1}(1)]/p^{t+1}, \quad t=1,2,\ldots$$

$$\text{and with } w^{1,1}(1) - c^{1,1}(1) > 0.$$

For every value of $w^{1,1}(1)>c^{1,1}(1)$ and by the use of (VII.10) we can generate a full sequence w (i.e. $w^{1,t}$ and $w^{2,t}$,t=1,2,...) satisfying the equilibrium conditions (VII.6) and (VII.7).

It remains only to verify whether at least one of such sequences of endowments satisfies that $w \in \mathbf{W}$. By assumption VII.2(c) the sequence c is uniformly bounded from below by some $\lambda > 0$. It is easy to check that for any sequence of endowments obtained from (VII.10), (VII.6) and (VII.7) such that

$$\text{(VII.11)} \qquad [w^{1,1}(1) - c^{1,1}(1)]/p^t < \lambda \quad \text{for } t=1,2,...$$

the consumption allocation c is a Walrasian equilibrium, but does not belong to the core by construction. It is now immediate that whenever $\text{Lim inf}_{t \to \infty} \|p(t)\| \geqq \epsilon > 0$ there exists some $w^{1,1}(1)$ satisfying (VII.11) such that $w^{1,1}(1) > c^{1,1}(1)$. This completes the proof for n=1.

The extension to the many commodities case is quite straightforward.

From Assumption VII.2 (b) we have that whenever $\text{Lim inf}_{t \to \infty} \|p(t)\| \geqq \epsilon > 0$ we have that $\text{Lim inf}_{t \to \infty} p(i,t) \geqq P \cdot \epsilon > 0$, i=1,...,n. Therefore we can chose $w^{j,t} = c^{j,t}$ for j=3,4,...,m and t=1,2,... and $w^{r,t}(i,t+s) = c^{r,t}(i,t+s)$ for r=1,2 , s=1,2, i=2,3,...,n, and t=1,2,... . Then our result for n=1 applies. QED.

Proposition VII.2 gives a sufficient condition for a competitive equilibrium to belong to the core of the economy. The interest of this result lies in the fact proven in Proposition VII.3 that competitive equilibria do not necessarily belong to the core. Moreover, the sufficiency condition given in Proposition VII.2 turns out to be critical. As proven by

Proposition VII.3 when this condition is not met one can always find reallocations of initial endowments across individuals of the same generation for which that consumption allocation still is a competitive equilibrium with the same equilibrium prices, but does not belong to the core.

From another point of view, Proposition VII.3 can be seen as a source of examples of Pareto optimum competitive equilibria that do not belong to the core of the economy. The example provided in Section VII.4 of a Pareto optimal competitive equilibrium not in the core is not exceptional.

We have already pointed out in the introduction that for Arrow-Debreu economies the classical set coincides with the Pareto set. Thus the standard results relating competitive equilibria, efficiency and core can be restated in terms of the classical set. Specifically, we can say that in Arrow-Debreu economies: i) all the allocations belonging to the classical set belong to the Pareto set (in fact the two sets coincide) and ii) all the allocations belonging to the classical set belong to the core for all the endowment allocations for which they can be implemented as competitive equilibria.

We shall now show that these two propositions hold true for overlapping generations economies. Thus the properties of overlapping generations economies turn out not to be radically different from Arrow-Debreu economies once the analysis is restricted to the classical set.

Proposition VII.4 Let Assumptions VII.1 and VII.2 be satisfied. Let c be a consumption allocation sequence belonging to the classical set, $c \in \mathbf{C}$. Then c is Pareto optimal.

Proof.- It follows immediately from our Proposition VII.1 and taking into account Balasko and Shell's [4] proposition that if the supporting prices of a weakly Pareto optimal consumption allocation satisfy that $\liminf_{t\to\infty}\|p(t)\| = 0$ then that consumption allocation is Pareto optimal. QED.

Proposition VII.5 Let Assumptions VII.1 and VII.2 be satisfied. Then the consumption allocation sequence c belongs to the core for every w for which it is a competitive equilibrium if and only if it belongs to the classical set, $c \in \mathbf{C}$.

Proof.- Proposition VII.1 establishes that the supporting prices of a consumption allocation sequence satisfy $\liminf_{t\to\infty}\|p(t)\|=0$ if and only if c belongs to the classical set. Thus, Propositions VII.1 and VII.2 together imply the sufficiency part, that is, if a consumption allocation belongs to the classical set it belongs to the core for all endowment sequences for which it is a competitive equilibrium. Further, Propositions VII.1 and VII.3 together imply the necessity part. Taken together, they say that if a consumption allocation does not belong to the classical set there exists an endowments allocation for which that consumption allocation does not belong to the core while still being a competitive equilibrium. QED.

VII.6 Monetary Equilibria and the Core

We have already pointed out that overlapping generations models have been considered as the most appropriate framework for the analysis of fiat money. It is thus natural to pay special attention to the relationship between monetary equilibria and core allocations. Besides the obvious relevance of our previous results to monetary equilibria we shall now introduce two additional resuls specifically referring to monetary allocations. We start by demonstrating that monetary equilibria with too much money will not belong to the core. But the main result of this section is that as we enlarge the economy by replication every monetary equilibrium becomes eventually excluded from the core.

With many consumers per generation we may have IOU equilibria, monetary equilibria, and a mixture of the two, i.e. simultaneously using IOUs and fiat money. The following result refers to economies in which in the long run all intertemporal purchases tend to be made for fiat money. This is an extreme case of a competitive equilibria in which not only is fiat money the only means of transferring purchasing power from present to the future, but money is present in all transactions. We show that these equilibria do not belong to the core.

Proposition VII.6 Let Assumption VII.1 be satisfied. Let c be a competitive equilibrium consumption allocation sequence and p the sequence of equilibrium prices. Then if

$$\text{(VII.12)} \qquad \liminf_{t\to\infty} p(t+1)\cdot|c^{\,t}(t+1)-w^{\,t}(t+1)|/M = 1\,,\ M>0\,,$$

the consumption allocation c does not belong to the core.

<u>Proof</u>.- From Definition VII.4 we know that

$$p(t+1)\cdot[c^{\,t}(t+1)-w^{\,t}(t+1)]=M,\quad t=0,1,2,\ldots\,.$$

Therefore, if (VII.12) is satisfied we have that

$$\liminf_{t\to\infty} p(t+1)\cdot|c^{\,t}(t+1)-w^{\,t}(t+1)|/p(t+1)\cdot[c^{\,t}(t+1)-w^{\,t}(t+1)]=1$$

Thus it must be that

$\text{Lim inf}_{t\to\infty} [c^{j,t}(t+1)-w^{j,t}(t+1)] =$

$\text{Lim inf}_{t\to\infty} |c^{j,t}(t+1)-w^{j,t}(t+1)| = z^j \geqq z > 0, \; j=1,\dots,m,$

where $z\epsilon\mathbb{R}^n_{++}$ and $z(i) = \min\{z^1(i),\dots,z^j(i),\dots,z^m(i)\}$, $i=1,\dots,n$.

Hence there exist T and λ, $0<\lambda\leqq z$ such that

$[c^{j,t}(t+1)-w^{j,t}(t+1)]\geqq\lambda$ for $j=1,\dots,m$ and $t=T,T+1,T+2,\dots$.

Consider now coalition S formed by agents (j,t) , $j=1,\dots,m$ and $t=T+1,T+2,\dots$ with the consumption allocation $\bar{c}$ such that

$$\bar{c}^{j,t} = c^{j,t} \quad \text{for all } (j,t)\epsilon S_t\text{ , } t=T+2,T+3,\dots \quad \text{and}$$

$$\bar{c}^{j,T+1} = [c^{j,T+1}(T+1)+\lambda \text{ , } c^{j,T+1}(T+2)], \quad j=1,\dots,m.$$

Allocation $\bar{c}$ is feasible for coalition S, is as good as c for all members of S and is strictly preferred by all members of S_{T+1}. Therefore, consumption allocation c does not belong to the core. QED.

This result seems to substantiate the interpretation given in Chapter VI that it is its role as a means of exchange rather than a store of value what confers social acceptability to fiat money. We have a case in which in the long run all the exchanges are intertemporal and made by the means of money. Thus, the proposition that no such equilibrium belongs to the core reinforces that view in a many agents economy.

Let us now give a general proposition refered to monetary equilibria. As the following Proposition shows, when the economy is enlarged by replication of the original economy no monetary equilibrium belongs to the core.

Proposition VII.7 Let ξ be an economy with m agents and n goods in which Assumptions VII.1 and VII.2(a) are satisfied. Let c be a monetary equilibrium consumption allocation of the economy ξ and p the equilibrium price sequence. Then, there exists K such that for the K-th replica of the economy $\xi(K)$, the consumption allocation c(K) does not belong to the core.

Proof.- Consider the k+1 replica of the economy and let S be a coalition formed by all agents (j,t), j=1,...,m, t=1,2,... , in $\xi(k+1)$ and all agents (j,0) , j=1,...,m, in $\xi(k)$. Since c is a monetary equilibrium we have that $p(1)\cdot[w^1(1)-c^1(1)]=M>0$. Therefore, there exists at least one vector $x^{j,1}(1)\in \mathbb{R}^n_+$ such that $p(1)\cdot[x^{j,1}(1)-c^{j,1}(1)]>0$, j=1,...,m, and $x^1(1)-w^1(1)\leq 0$. Consider now the consumption allocation $\bar{c}$ for the members of coalition S such that $\bar{c}^{j,t}=c^{j,t}$ for all $(j,t)\in S_t$, t=0,2,3,... and $\bar{c}^{j,1}=[(x^{j,1}(1)+kc^{j,1}(1))/(k+1)\ ,\ c^{j,1}(2)]$ for all $(j,t)\in S_1$.

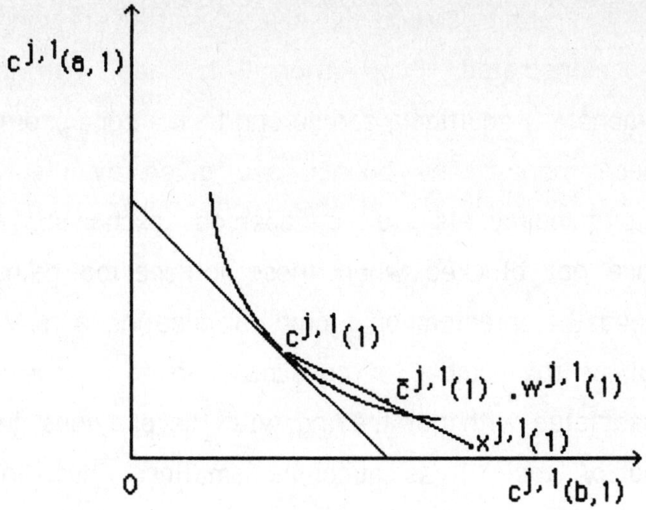

Figure VII.2

Observe that $\bar{c}$ is obtained as a linear convex combination of vectors $c^{j,1}$ and $\tilde{c}^{j,1} = [x^{j,1}(1), c^{j,1}(2)]$ and that as k becomes large $\bar{c}^{j,1} \rightarrow c^{j,1}$. Thus, we have that

$$p(1)\cdot \bar{c}^{j,1}(1) + p(2)\cdot\bar{c}^{j,1}(2) \geq p(1)\cdot c^{j,1}(1) + p(2)\cdot c^{j,1}(2), \quad j=1,\ldots,m.$$

Moreover, it is easy to check that consumption allocation $\bar{c}$ is feasible.

By Assumptions 1 and 2(a) there exists a finite K such that

$$u^{j,1}\left[(x^{j,1}(1)+Kc^{j,1}(1))/(K+1)\ ,\ c^{j,1}(2)\right] > u^{j,1}\left[c^{j,1}(1), c^{j,1}(2)\right],$$

$j=1,\ldots,m.$

See Figure 2. Since $\bar{c}^{j,t} = c^{j,t}$ for the rest of members of S, S will block consumption allocation c. QED.

The intuition behind this result is the following. In Chapter V we have demonstrated, Proposition V.1, that with one agent per generation monetary equilibria can belong to the core provided they do not use too much money. The bounds are given by the value implicitly attributed by individuals to intraperiod exchange. Thus monetary equilibria are not blocked when these intraperiod gains from trading always exceed the intertemporal gain of creating a new currency. It is obvious that, as the number of consumers in each generation increases, the loss associated with not trading with the previous generation in the first period of their lives becomes smaller. Thus, in the limit the intraperiod costs become nill for each generation and no monetary equilibrium can belong to the core of the economy.

This proposition can be interpreted as a formal proof of the observation by Clower that money is not held as the result of individual voluntary choice but by social contrivance, as pointed out in the Introduction.

VII.7 Final Remarks on Some Topics in Monetary Theory

In this section of final remarks we wish to discuss in some detail the implications of our results for some of the current topics in modern general equilibrium monetary theory. We shall focus on two areas: monetary theory in overlapping generations models, as developed in Grandmont[31], Kareken and Wallace [39], and Sargent[54], among many others, and the role of money in giving trustworthiness to intertemporal allocations, as studied by Douglas Gale[28] and [29].

Monetary equilibria as studied in Chapter VI pose a specific type of problem. Even with one agent per generation, Pareto optimal monetary equilibria may not belong to the core. Moreover, if we stick at the standard one-good model in which fiat money is analysed, no monetary equilibrium belongs to the core. This result can be interpreted as accounting for the fact that, in the absence of other forms of trade, every generation has an incentive to reject the money carried over by the former generation creating its own money instead. With many goods, dynamically efficient monetary equilibria can be in the core if accompanied by a sufficient amount of intergenerational barter, i.e. if the utility gains derived from barter with the former generation fully compensate for the loss incurred in accepting its money. All this is proved in Chapter VI. But we have just seen that these results are no longer true for economies with many agents per generation. With many agents, refusing the money held by the previous generation does not necessarily entail foregoing any form of intra-period exchange. Agents heading a blocking coalition can always reallocate goods with members of their own generation. The utility loss from not trading with the previous generation is made smaller by enlarging the number of agents in each generation. Hence, as generations become large, the utility losses associated with blocking become small and are ultimately outweighed by the utility gains derived from repudiating the existing money. Indeed we demonstrate that as the economy is enlarged by replication monetary equilibria cease to belong to the core and in the limit all become excluded.

All these results appear to be negative with respect to the important literature on fiat money in overlapping generations economies. However, our results can be interpreted in a more positive spirit as providing a rigorous demonstration of the claim made by Clower [19] that the social acceptance of money is not voluntary and based on its virtue of being a store of value. As a matter of fact, there is nothing terrible or new in this view of money. Douglas Gale [28] and [29] when examining the role of money in the social acceptance of allocations, points out that «it is not the invention of paper money which restores trustworthiness. The Walras allocations are trustworthy in the monetary economy only because there is, in the background, a government which can enforce, evidently at no cost, the payment of [money] taxes. Thus, we have introduced not just a new commodity (money) but a new social institution »(p.465). From this point of view it is obvious that fiat money has been introduced in overlapping generations models as a commodity and not as a social institution. In this respect, de Vries [58] has recently examined the case in which the acceptance of fiat money is made compulsory, i.e. money is given the status of "legal tender".

Let us be more specific in comparing our results with Douglas Gale's [28] work. As we have already pointed out, he has shown that the introduction of money may help in making socially acceptable allocations which would have been blocked without its help. In Gale's model there is a finite number of periods and, being an Arrow-Debreu economy in every respect, competitive equilibria belong to the core of the economy. However, he argues that in those equilibria in which there is net borrowing and lending, lenders have good reasons not to trust borrowers. It is in their interest to break the futures contracts in later periods of their lives. Gale thus defines the concept of sequential core, i.e. those allocations which belong to the core both in the first and in the subsequent periods, and shows that an allocation is trustworthy if and only if it belongs to the sequential core. Thus, lenders would not trust allocations out of the sequential core even if they belong to the core of the economy. In order to circumvent this problem he proposes that the social institution of money may render otherwise untrustworthy allocations worth the trust. As in all finite horizon monetary models he needs to introduce a money tax at the end period in order make money valuable. He then finds that in this economy competitive monetary equilibria do belong to the sequential core.

From this point of view, our results can be interpreted in the following way. It seems natural to reconsider his problem in an overlapping generations economy in which one does not need the device of the money tax in order to make money valuable. Then, our findings that Pareto optimal monetary competitive equilibria might not belong to the core and that when the economy becomes large by replication no monetary allocation belongs to the core seem to confirm Gale's assertion that what makes allocations socially stable in his model is not the introduction of fiat money, but making money taxes compulsory.

We can go deeper in comparing our model with Douglas Gale's. We have already pointed out that in order to show that equilibrium allocations involving net borrowing or lending might not be trustworthy he needs to assume that agents can break their futures contracts at later dates. As we shall now argue our results can be seen as providing a rationale for Gale's assumption on agents not honouring their contracts.

Let us start by noting that an IOU equilibrium in an overlapping generations model can be understood as a sequence of overlapping finite horizon Gale's competitive equilibria. Let us develop this point and focus on IOU competitive equilibria. While there is borrowing and lending, in the IOU equilibrium there is no income transfer across generations. Further, observe that in those equilibria contracts in the futures markets are signed on the two sides by consumers belonging to the same generation. Therefore, as far as the futures markets are concerned, IOU equilibria can be seen as a sequence of isolated generations, i.e. as a sequence of overlapping two-period Gale's equilibria. Alternatively, Gale's model can be considered as isolating one single generation of an IOU equilibrium sequence from an overlapping generations model in order to examine their behaviour in the futures market.

In spite of their similarity, the two models seem to yield different results. While in Gale's model all competitive equilibria belong to the core, in our model their equivalent, i.e. our IOU equilibria, do not. Thus, the fact of placing a collection of selfcontained economies one after the other breaks the relation between competitive equilibria and core. In other words, from a game theoretical point of view it makes a substantial difference to consider an isolated finite chain of periods or the full infinite sequence. As we have seen in Proposition VII.3 only those walrasian equilibria in which there is no borrowing and lending in the long run are always in the core. Hence, the core of an overlapping generations economy formed by chaining a sequence of Gale's two period economies would not contain the allocations that do not belong to the sequential core in Gale's model. Therefore, one need not suppose that agents do not honour their contracts to claim that equilibria which involve borrowing might not be viable. The mere fact that agents live in an endless chain of generations can make IOU equilibria untrustworthy. Our results can thus be considered as a rationale for using the concept of sequential core when one analyses the viability of allocations in finite horizon economies.

Notes to Chapter VII

1 The model can be trivially generalized to a variable number of agents per generation $m(t)$ uniformly bounded above by a finite number m.

2 As proven by Millan [44] Balasko and Shell's [4] characterization of Pareto optimal allocations can be extended to economies with many agents. Note that Burke [10] has shown that the assumption on the boundedness of the Gaussian curvatures is quite unnecessary.

3 Note that $S_{f-1} = \emptyset$ and hence for the first generation the feasibility condition reads

$$\sum_{j \in S_f} c^{j,f}(f) = \sum_{j \in S_f} w^{j,f}(f).$$

4 Kovenock [43] has produced another example of a Pareto optimum walrasian equilibrium not in the core while the set of core allocations is empty. In his example the two agents of any generation have preferences defined on different goods. Only the two members of generation $t=0$ share their preferences for one common good.

5 Observe that our result is stronger than Chae's [16] Theorem 4.1, where with a continuum of agents he finds that a sufficient condition for an allocation to belong to the core is that the present value of the total endowment be finite.

References

1. K. Arrow and F. Hahn, General Competitive Analysis, Holden-Day, San Francisco, 1971.

2. R.J. Aumann and J.H. Drèze, Cooperative Games with Coalition Structures, International Journal of Game Theory III (1974), 217-237.

3. Y. Balasko, D. Cass and K. Shell, Existence of Competitive Equilibrium in a General Overlapping Generations Model, Journal of Economic Theory, 23 (1980), 307-322.

4. Y. Balasko and K. Shell, The Overlapping Generations Model , I : The Case of Pure Exchange without Money , Journal of Economic Theory, 23 (1980), 281-306.

5. Y. Balasko and K. Shell, The Overlapping Generations Model, II : The Case of Pure Exchange with Money, Journal of Economic Theory, 24 (1981), 112-142.

6. Y. Balasko and K. Shell, The Overlapping-Generations Model. III. The case of log-linear utility functions, Journal of Economic Theory 24 (1981), 143-152.

7. Y. Balasko and K. Shell, Lump-Sum Taxes and Transfers: Public Debt in the Overlapping-Generations Model, in Equilibrium Analysis: Essays in Honor of Kenneth J. Arrow, Vol.2 (W.P. Heller, R.M. Starr, and D. A. Starrett, eds.), Cambridge University Press, Cambridge, 1986.

8. L.M. Benveniste and D. Cass,"On the Existence of Optimal Stationary Equilibria with a Fixed Supply of Fiat Money:I. The Case of a Single Consumer", Journal of Political Economy, 94 (1986), 402-417.

9. J. Bryant, Transaction Demand for Money and Moral Hazard, in J.H. Kareken and N. Wallace [27] (1980), 233-241.

10. J. Burke, Inactive Transfer Policies and Efficiency in General Overlapping Generations Economies, Journal of Mathematical

Economics 16 (1987), 201-222.

11. D. Cass, On Capital Overaccumulation in the Aggregative Neoclassical Model of Economic Growth: A Complete Characterization, Journal of Economic Theory 4 (1972), 200-223.

12. D. Cass, M. Okuno and I. Zilcha, The Role of Money in Supporting the Pareto Optimality of Competitive Equilibrium in Consumption-Loan Type Models, Journal of Economic Theory 20 (1979), 41-80.

13. D. Cass and K. Shell, In Defense of a Basic Approach, in J.H. Kareken and N. Wallace [27] (1980), 251-260.

14. D. Cass and M. Yaari, A Re-examination of the Pure Consumption Loans Model, Journal of Political Economy 74 (1966), 353-367.

15. D. Cass and M. Yaari, Individual Saving, Aggregate Capital Accumulation and Efficient Growth, in Essays on the Theory of Optimal Economic Growth, (K. Shell, ed.), The MIT Press, Cambridge Mass, 1967.

16. S. Chae, Short Run Core Equivalence in an Overlapping Generations Model, Journal of Economic Theory, 43 (1987), 170-183.

17. S. Chae and J. Esteban, The Bounded Core of an Overlapping Generations Economy, International Economic Review, 30 (1989), 519-526.

18. R.W. Clower, A Reconsideration of the Microfoundations of Monetary Theory, Western Economic Journal 6 (1967), 1-9.

19. R.W. Clower, Introduction, in R.W. Clower (ed.), Monetary Theory, Penguin Books, Hamondsworth, 1969, 7-21.

20. G. Debreu, Economies with a Finite Set of Equilibria, Econometrica, 38 (1970), pp.387-393.

21. P.A. Diamond, National Debt in a Neoclassical Growth Model,

American Economic Review 55 (1965), 1126-1150.

22. J. Esteban, A Characterization of the Core in Overlapping Generations Economies, Journal of Economic Theory, 39 (1986), 439-456.

23. J. Esteban, "Core, Bounded Core and Efficiency in Overlapping Generations Economies", in B. Dutta (ed.), Theoretical Issues in Development Economics, Oxford University Press, (forthcoming 1992).

24. J. Esteban and T. Millan, Competitive Equilibria and the Core Of Overlapping Generations Economies, Journal of Economic Theory 50 (1990), 155-174.

25. J. Esteban, T. Mitra and D. Ray, Monetary Equilibria with Positive Outside Money in the Overlapping Generations Model, unpublished manuscript (1988).

26. J.Esteban, T. Mitra and D. Ray, On the Existence of Efficient Monetary Equilibria, unpublished manuscript, (1989).

27. David Gale, Pure Exchange Equilibrium of Dynamic Economic Models, Journal of Economic Theory 6 (1973), 12-36.

28. Douglas Gale, The Core of an Economy without Trust, Journal of Economic Theory 19, (1978), 456-491.

29. Douglas Gale, Money: in Equilibrium, Cambridge University Press, Cambridge, 1982.

30. J.D. Geanakoplos and H.M. Polemarchakis, Intertemporally Separable, Overlapping-Generations Economies, Journal of Economic Theory 34 (1984), 207-215.

31. J.M. Grandmont, Money and Value, Cambridge University Press, Cambridge, 1983.

32. J.M. Grandmont, On Endogenous Competitive Business Cycles, Econometrica 53 (1985), 995-1045.

33. S. Grossman, A Characterization of the Optimality of Equilibrium in Incomplete Markets, Journal of Economic Theory, 15 (1977), 1-15.

34. F.H. Hahn, Money and Inflation, Basil Blackwell, Oxford, 1982.

35. O. Hart, On the Optimality of Equilibrium When the Market Structure is Incomplete, Journal of Economic Theory 11 (1975), 418-443.

36. K. Hendricks, K. Judd and D. Kovenock , A Note on the Core of the Overlapping Generations Model, Economic Letters 6, (1980), 95-97.

37. M. Kaneko and M. Wooders, The Core of a Game with a Continuum of Players and Finite Coalitions :The model and some results, IMA Preprint no.111 (1984), Institute for Mathematics and its Applications,University of Minnesota.

38. M. Kaneko and M. Wooders, The core of a Game with a Continuum of Players and Finite Coalitions : Nonemptiness with Bounded Sizes of Coalitions, Department of Economics, University of Toronto, W.P. #8503 , (1985).

39. J. Kareken and N. Wallace (eds.), Models of Monetary Economies , Federal Reserve Bank of Minneapolis, Minneapolis, 1980.

40. T.J. Kehoe and D.K. Levine, Intertemporal Separability in Overlapping Generations Models, Journal of Economic Theory 34 (1984) , 216-226.

41. T.J. Kehoe and D.K. Levine, Regularity in Overlapping Generations Exchange Economies, Journal of Mathematical Economics 13 (1984), 69-93.

42. T.J. Kehoe and D.K. Levine, "Comparative Statics and Perfect Foresight in Infinite Horizon Economies", Econometrica , 53 (1985), pp. 433-453.

43. D. Kovenock, A Second Note on the Core of the overlapping generations Model, Economic Letters 14 , (1984) , 101-106.

44. T. Millan, On the Existence of Optimal Competitive Equilibria in the Overlapping Generations Model, Ph.D. Thesis, University of Minnesota, (1981).

45. T. Mitra, Public Debt in the Overlapping Generations Model: A Characterization of Bonafide Tax-Transfers Policies, unpublished manuscript, 1987.

46. R.B. Myerson, Graphs and Cooperation in Games, Math. of Operations Research 2 (1977), 225-229.

47. M. Okuno and I. Zilcha, On the Efficiency of a Competitive Equilibrium in Infinite Horizon Monetary Economies, Review of Economic Studies 47 (1980),797-807.

48. M. Okuno and I. Zilcha, A Proof of Existence of Competitive Equilibrium in a Generation-Overlapping Exchange Economy with Money, International Economic Review 22 (1981), 239-252.

49. D. Patinkin, Money, Interest and Prices, 2nd. edition, Harper and Row, New York, 1965.

50. P.A. Samuelson, An Exact Consumption-Loan Model of Interest with or without the Social Contrivance of Money, Journal of Political Economy 66, (1958), 467-482.

51. P.A. Samuelson, Optimum Social Security in a Life-Cycle Growth Model, International Economic Review 16 (1975), 539-544.

52. M. Santos, Existence of Equilibria for Monetary Economies, International Economic Review 31, (1990), forthcoming.

53. M. Santos and J. Bona, On the Structure of the Equilibrium Price Set of Overlapping-Generations Economies, Journal of Mathematical Economics, 19 (1989), 209-230 .

54. T. Sargent, Dynamic Macroeconomic Theory, Harvard University Press, Cambridge, Mass., (1987).

55. K. Shell, Notes on the Economics of Infinity, Journal of Political Economy, 79 (1971), 1002-1011.

56. M. Shubik, Society, Land, Love or Money, A Strategic Model of How to Glue the Generations Together, Journal of Economic Behavior and Organization 2 (1981), 359-385.

57. M. Shubik, A Game-Theoretical Approach to Political Economy, The MIT Press, Cambridge (Mass.), 1985.

58. C.G. de Vries, Legal Tender and the Value of Money, mimeo, Erasmus University Rotterdam, (1984).

59. N. Wallace, The Overlapping Generations Model of Fiat Money, in Kareken and Wallace [27] (1980), 49-82.

Lecture Notes in Economics and Mathematical Systems

For information about Vols. 1–210
please contact your bookseller or Springer-Verlag

Vol. 211: P. van den Heuvel, The Stability of a Macroeconomic System with Quantity Constraints. VII, 169 pages. 1983.

Vol. 212: R. Sato and T. Nôno, Invariance Principles and the Structure of Technology. V, 94 pages. 1983.

Vol. 213: Aspiration Levels in Bargaining and Economic Decision Making. Proceedings, 1982. Edited by R. Tietz. VIII, 406 pages. 1983.

Vol. 214: M. Faber, H. Niemes und G. Stephan, Entropie, Umweltschutz und Rohstoffverbrauch. IX, 181 Seiten. 1983.

Vol. 215: Semi-Infinite Programming and Applications. Proceedings, 1981. Edited by A.V. Fiacco and K.O. Kortanek. XI, 322 pages. 1983.

Vol. 216: H.H. Müller, Fiscal Policies in a General Equilibrium Model with Persistent Unemployment. VI, 92 pages. 1983.

Vol. 217: Ch. Grootaert, The Relation Between Final Demand and Income Distribution. XIV, 105 pages. 1983.

Vol 218: P. van Loon, A Dynamic Theory of the Firm: Production, Finance and Investment. VII, 191 pages. 1983.

Vol. 219: E. van Damme, Refinements of the Nash Equilibrium Concept. VI. 151 pages. 1983.

Vol. 220: M. Aoki, Notes on Economic Time Series Analysis: System Theoretic Perspectives. IX, 249 pages. 1983.

Vol. 221: S. Nakamura, An Inter-Industry Translog Model of Prices and Technical Change for the West German Economy. XIV, 290 pages. 1984.

Vol. 222: P. Meier, Energy Systems Analysis for Developing Countries. VI, 344 pages. 1984.

Vol. 223: W. Trockel, Market Demand. VIII, 205 pages. 1984.

Vol. 224: M. Kiy, Ein disaggregiertes Prognosesystem fur die Bundesrepublik Deutschland. XVIII, 276 Seiten. 1984.

Vol. 225: T.R. von Ungern-Sternberg, Zur Analyse von Märkten mit unvollständiger Nachfragerinformaton. IX, 125 Seiten. 1984.

Vol. 226: Selected Topics in Operations Research and Mathematical Economics. Proceedings, 1963. Edited by G. Hammer and D. Pallaschke IX, 478 pages. 1984.

Vol. 227: Risk and Capital. Proceedings, 1983. Edited by G. Bamberg and K. Spremann VII, 306 pages. 1984.

Vol. 228: Nonlinear Models of Fluctuating Growth. Proceedings, 1983. Edited by R.M. Goodwin, M. Krüger and A. Vercelli. XVII, 277 pages. 1984.

Vol. 229: Interactive Decision Analysis. Proceedings, 1983. Edited by M. Grauer and A.P. Wierzbicki. VIII, 269 pages. 1984.

Vol. 230: Macro-Economic Planning with Conflicting Goals. Proceedings, 1982. Edited by M. Despontin, P. Nijkamp and J. Spronk. VI, 297 pages. 1984.

Vol. 231: G.F. Newell, The M/M/8 Service System with Ranked Servers in Heavy Traffic. XI, 126 pages. 1984.

Vol. 232: L. Bauwens, Bayesian Full Information Analysis of Simultaneous Equation Models Using Integration by Monte Carlo. VI, 114 pages. 1984.

Vol. 233: G. Wagenhals, The World Copper Market. XI, 190 pages. 1984.

Vol. 234: B.C. Eaves, A Course in Triangulations for Solving Equations with Deformations. III, 302 pages. 1984.

Vol. 235: Stochastic Models in Reliability Theory Proceedings, 1984. Edited by S. Osaki and Y. Hatoyama. VII, 212 pages. 1984.

Vol. 236: G. Gandolfo, P.C. Padoan, A Disequilibrium Model of Real and Financial Accumulation in an Open Economy. VI, 172 pages. 1984.

Vol. 237: Misspecification Analysis. Proceedings, 1983. Edited by T.K. Dijkstra. V, 129 pages. 1984.

Vol. 238: W. Domschke, A. Drexl, Location and Layout Planning. IV, 134 pages. 1985.

Vol. 239: Microeconomic Models of Housing Markets. Edited by K. Stahl. VII, 197 pages. 1985.

Vol. 240: Contributions to Operations Research. Proceedings, 1984. Edited by K. Neumann and D. Pallaschke. V, 190 pages. 1985.

Vol. 241: U. Wittmann, Das Konzept rationaler Preiserwartungen. XI, 310 Seiten. 1985.

Vol. 242: Decision Making with Multiple Objectives. Proceedings, 1984. Edited by Y.Y. Haimes and V. Chankong. XI, 571 pages. 1985.

Vol. 243: Integer Programming and Related Areas. A Classified Bibliography 1981–1984. Edited by R. von Randow. XX, 386 pages. 1985.

Vol. 244: Advances in Equilibrium Theory. Proceedings, 1984. Edited by C.D. Aliprantis, O. Burkinshaw and N.J. Rothman. II, 235 pages. 1985.

Vol. 245: J.E.M. Wilhelm, Arbitrage Theory. VII, 114 pages. 1985.

Vol. 246: P.W. Otter, Dynamic Feature Space Modelling, Filtering and Self-Tuning Control of Stochastic Systems. XIV, 177 pages.1985.

Vol. 247: Optimization and Discrete Choice in Urban Systems. Proceedings, 1983. Edited by B.G. Hutchinson, P. Nijkamp and M. Batty VI, 371 pages. 1985.

Vol. 248: Pural Rationality and Interactive Decision Processes. Proceedings, 1984. Edited by M. Grauer, M. Thompson and A.P. Wierzbicki. VI, 354 pages. 1985.

Vol. 249: Spatial Price Equilibrium: Advances in Theory, Computation and Application. Proceedings, 1984. Edited by P.T. Harker. VII, 277 pages. 1985.

Vol. 250: M. Roubens, Ph. Vincke, Preference Modelling. VIII, 94 pages. 1985.

Vol. 251: Input-Output Modeling. Proceedings, 1984. Edited by A. Smyshlyaev. VI, 261 pages. 1985.

Vol. 252: A. Birolini, On the Use of Stochastic Processes in Modeling Reliability Problems. VI, 105 pages. 1985.

Vol. 253: C. Withagen, Economic Theory and International Trade in Natural Exhaustible Resources. VI, 172 pages. 1985.

Vol. 254: S. Müller, Arbitrage Pricing of Contingent Claims. VIII, 151 pages. 1985.

Vol. 255: Nondifferentiable Optimization: Motivations and Applications. Proceedings, 1984. Edited by V.F. Demyanov and D. Pallaschke. VI, 350 pages. 1985.

Vol. 256: Convexity and Duality in Optimization. Proceedings, 1984. Edited by J. Ponstein. V, 142 pages. 1985.

Vol. 257: Dynamics of Macrosystems. Proceedings, 1984. Edited by J.-P. Aubin, D. Saari and K. Sigmund. VI, 280 pages. 1985.

Vol. 258: H. Funke, Eine allgemeine Theorie der Polypol- und Oligopolpreisbildung. III, 237 pages. 1985.

Vol. 259: Infinite Programming. Proceedings, 1984. Edited by E.J. Anderson and A.B. Philpott. XIV, 244 pages. 1985.

Vol. 260: H.-J. Kruse, Degeneracy Graphs and the Neighbourhood Problem. VIII, 128 pages. 1986.

Vol. 261: Th.R. Gulledge, Jr., N.K. Womer, The Economics of Made-to-Order Production. VI, 134 pages. 1986.

Vol. 262: H.U. Buhl, A Neo-Classical Theory of Distribution and Wealth. V, 146 pages. 1986.

Vol. 263: M. Schäfer, Resource Extraction and Market Struucture. XI, 154 pages. 1986.

Vol. 264: Models of Economic Dynamics. Proceedings, 1983. Edited by H.F. Sonnenschein. VII, 212 pages. 1986.

Vol. 265: Dynamic Games and Applications in Economics. Edited by T. Basar. IX, 288 pages. 1986.

Vol. 266: Multi-Stage Production Planning and Inventory Control. Edited by S. Axsäter, Ch. Schneeweiss and E. Silver. V, 264 pages.1986.

Vol. 267: R. Bemelmans, The Capacity Aspect of Inventories. IX, 165 pages. 1986.

Vol. 268: V. Firchau, Information Evaluation in Capital Markets. VII, 103 pages. 1986.

Vol. 269: A. Borglin, H. Keiding, Optimality in Infinite Horizon Economies. VI, 180 pages. 1986.

Vol. 270: Technological Change, Employment and Spatial Dynamics. Proceedings, 1985. Edited by P. Nijkamp. VII, 466 pages. 1986.

Vol. 271: C. Hildreth, The Cowles Commission in Chicago, 1939–1955. V, 176 pages. 1986.

Vol. 272: G. Clemenz, Credit Markets with Asymmetric Information. VIII,212 pages. 1986.

Vol. 273: Large-Scale Modelling and Interactive Decision Analysis. Proceedings, 1985. Edited by G. Fandel, M. Grauer, A. Kurzhanski and A.P. Wierzbicki. VII, 363 pages. 1986.

Vol. 274: W.K. Klein Haneveld, Duality in Stochastic Linear and Dynamic Programming. VII, 295 pages. 1986.

Vol. 275: Competition, Instability, and Nonlinear Cycles. Proceedings, 1985. Edited by W. Semmler. XII, 340 pages. 1986.

Vol. 276: M.R. Baye, D.A. Black, Consumer Behavior, Cost of Living Measures, and the Income Tax. VII, 119 pages. 1986.

Vol. 277: Studies in Austrian Capital Theory, Investment and Time. Edited by M. Faber. VI, 317 pages. 1986.

Vol. 278: W.E. Diewert, The Measurement of the Economic Benefits of Infrastructure Services. V, 202 pages. 1986.

Vol. 279: H.-J. Büttler, G. Frei and B. Schips, Estimation of Disequilibrium Modes. VI, 114 pages. 1986.

Vol. 280: H.T. Lau, Combinatorial Heuristic Algorithms with FORTRAN. VII, 126 pages. 1986.

Vol. 281: Ch.-L. Hwang, M.-J. Lin, Group Decision Making under Multiple Criteria. XI, 400 pages. 1987.

Vol. 282: K. Schittkowski, More Test Examples for Nonlinear Programming Codes. V, 261 pages. 1987.

Vol. 283: G. Gabisch, H.-W. Lorenz, Business Cycle Theory. VII, 229 pages. 1987.

Vol. 284: H. Lütkepohl, Forecasting Aggregated Vector ARMA Processes. X, 323 pages. 1987.

Vol. 285: Toward Interactive and Intelligent Decision Support Systems. Volume 1. Proceedings, 1986. Edited by Y. Sawaragi, K. Inoue and H. Nakayama. XII, 445 pages. 1987.

Vol. 286: Toward Interactive and Intelligent Decision Support Systems. Volume 2. Proceedings, 1986. Edited by Y. Sawaragi, K. Inoue and H. Nakayama. XII, 450 pages. 1987.

Vol. 287: Dynamical Systems. Proceedings, 1985. Edited by A.B. Kurzhanski and K. Sigmund. VI, 215 pages. 1987.

Vol. 288: G.D. Rudebusch, The Estimation of Macroeconomic Disequilibrium Models with Regime Classification Information. VII,128 pages. 1987.

Vol. 289: B.R. Meijboom, Planning in Decentralized Firms. X, 168 pages. 1987.

Vol. 290: D.A. Carlson, A. Haurie, Infinite Horizon Optimal Control. XI, 254 pages. 1987.

Vol. 291: N. Takahashi, Design of Adaptive Organizations. VI, 140 pages. 1987.

Vol. 292: I. Tchijov, L. Tomaszewicz (Eds.), Input-Output Modeling. Proceedings, 1985. VI, 195 pages. 1987.

Vol. 293: D. Batten, J. Casti, B. Johansson (Eds.), Economic Evolution and Structural Adjustment. Proceedings, 1985. VI, 382 pages.

Vol. 294: J. Jahn, W. Knabs (Eds.), Recent Advances and Historical Development of Vector Optimization. VII, 405 pages. 1987.

Vol. 295. H. Meister, The Purification Problem for Constrained Games with Incomplete Information. X, 127 pages. 1987.

Vol. 296: A. Börsch-Supan, Econometric Analysis of Discrete Choice. VIII, 211 pages. 1987.

Vol. 297: V. Fedorov, H. Läuter (Eds.), Model-Oriented Data Analysis. Proceedings, 1987. VI, 239 pages. 1988.

Vol. 298: S.H. Chew, Q. Zheng, Integral Global Optimization. VII, 179 pages. 1988.

Vol. 299: K. Marti, Descent Directions and Efficient Solutions in Discretely Distributed Stochastic Programs. XIV, 178 pages. 1988.

Vol. 300: U. Derigs, Programming in Networks and Graphs. XI, 315 pages. 1988.

Vol. 301: J. Kacprzyk, M. Roubens (Eds.), Non-Conventional Preference Relations in Decision Making. VII, 155 pages. 1988.

Vol. 302: H.A. Eiselt, G. Pederzoli (Eds.), Advances in Optimization and Control. Proceedings, 1986. VIII, 372 pages. 1988.

Vol. 303: F.X. Diebold, Empirical Modeling of Exchange Rate Dynamics. VII, 143 pages. 1988.

Vol. 304: A. Kurzhanski, K. Neumann, D. Pallaschke (Eds.), Optimization, Parallel Processing and Applications. Proceedings, 1987. VI, 292 pages. 1988.

Vol. 305: G.-J.C.Th. van Schijndel, Dynamic Firm and Investor Behaviour under Progressive Personal Taxation. X, 215 pages.1988.

Vol. 306: Ch. Klein, A Static Microeconomic Model of Pure Competition. VIII, 139 pages. 1988.

Vol. 307: T.K. Dijkstra (Ed.), On Model Uncertainty and its Statistical Implications. VII, 138 pages. 1988.

Vol. 308: J.R. Daduna, A. Wren (Eds.), Computer-Aided Transit Scheduling. VIII, 339 pages. 1988.

Vol. 309: G. Ricci, K. Velupillai (Eds.), Growth Cycles and Multisectoral Economics: the Goodwin Tradition. III, 126 pages. 1988.

Vol. 310: J. Kacprzyk, M. Fedrizzi (Eds.), Combining Fuzzy Imprecision with Probabilistic Uncertainty in Decision Making. IX, 399 pages. 1988.

Vol. 311: R. Färe, Fundamentals of Production Theory. IX, 163 pages. 1988.

Vol. 312: J. Krishnakumar, Estimation of Simultaneous Equation Models with Error Components Structure. X, 357 pages. 1988.

Vol. 313: W. Jammernegg, Sequential Binary Investment Decisions. VI, 156 pages. 1988.

Vol. 314: R. Tietz, W. Albers, R. Selten (Eds.), Bounded Rational Behavior in Experimental Games and Markets. VI, 368 pages. 1988.

Vol. 315: I. Orishimo, G.J.D. Hewings, P. Nijkamp (Eds), Information Technology: Social and Spatial Perspectives. Proceedings 1986. VI, 268 pages. 1988.

Vol. 316: R.L. Basmann, D.J. Slottje, K. Hayes, J.D. Johnson, D.J. Molina, The Generalized Fechner-Thurstone Direct Utility Function and Some of its Uses. VIII, 159 pages. 1988.

Vol. 317: L. Bianco, A. La Bella (Eds.), Freight Transport Planning and Logistics. Proceedings, 1987. X, 568 pages. 1988.

Vol. 318: T. Doup, Simplicial Algorithms on the Simplotope. VIII, 262 pages. 1988.

Vol. 319: D.T. Luc, Theory of Vector Optimization. VIII, 173 pages. 1989.

Vol. 320: D. van der Wijst, Financial Structure in Small Business. VII, 181 pages. 1989.

Vol. 321: M. Di Matteo, R.M. Goodwin, A. Vercelli (Eds.), Technological and Social Factors in Long Term Fluctuations. Proceedings. IX, 442 pages. 1989.

Vol. 322: T. Kollintzas (Ed.), The Rational Expectations Equilibrium Inventory Model. XI, 269 pages. 1989.

Vol. 323: M.B.M. de Koster, Capacity Oriented Analysis and Design of Production Systems. XII, 245 pages. 1989.

Vol. 324: I.M. Bomze, B.M. Pötscher, Game Theoretical Foundations of Evolutionary Stability. VI, 145 pages. 1989.

Vol. 325: P. Ferri, E. Greenberg, The Labor Market and Business Cycle Theories. X, 183 pages. 1989.

Vol. 326: Ch. Sauer, Alternative Theories of Output, Unemployment, and Inflation in Germany: 1960–1985. XIII, 206 pages. 1989.

Vol. 327: M. Tawada, Production Structure and International Trade. V, 132 pages. 1989.

Vol. 328: W. Güth, B. Kalkofen, Unique Solutions for Strategic Games. VII, 200 pages. 1989.

Vol. 329: G. Tillmann, Equity, Incentives, and Taxation. VI, 132 pages. 1989.

Vol. 330: P.M. Kort, Optimal Dynamic Investment Policies of a Value Maximizing Firm. VII, 185 pages. 1989.

Vol. 331: A. Lewandowski, A.P. Wierzbicki (Eds.), Aspiration Based Decision Support Systems. X, 400 pages. 1989.

Vol. 332: T.R. Gulledge, Jr., L.A. Litteral (Eds.), Cost Analysis Applications of Economics and Operations Research. Proceedings. VII, 422 pages. 1989.

Vol. 333: N. Dellaert, Production to Order. VII, 158 pages. 1989.

Vol. 334: H.-W. Lorenz, Nonlinear Dynamical Economics and Chaotic Motion. XI, 248 pages. 1989.

Vol. 335: A.G. Lockett, G. Islei (Eds.), Improving Decision Making in Organisations. Proceedings. IX, 606 pages. 1989.

Vol. 336: T. Puu, Nonlinear Economic Dynamics. VII, 119 pages. 1989.

Vol. 337: A. Lewandowski, I. Stanchev (Eds.), Methodology and Software for Interactive Decision Support. VIII, 309 pages. 1989.

Vol. 338: J.K. Ho, R.P. Sundarraj, DECOMP: an Implementation of Dantzig-Wolfe Decomposition for Linear Programming. VI, 206 pages.

Vol. 339: J. Terceiro Lomba, Estimation of Dynamic Econometric Models with Errors in Variables. VIII, 116 pages. 1990.

Vol. 340: T. Vasko, R. Ayres, L. Fontvieille (Eds.), Life Cycles and Long Waves. XIV, 293 pages. 1990.

Vol. 341: G.R. Uhlich, Descriptive Theories of Bargaining. IX, 165 pages. 1990.

Vol. 342: K. Okuguchi, F. Szidarovszky, The Theory of Oligopoly with Multi-Product Firms. V, 167 pages. 1990.

Vol. 343: C. Chiarella, The Elements of a Nonlinear Theory of Economic Dynamics. IX, 149 pages. 1990.

Vol. 344: K. Neumann, Stochastic Project Networks. XI, 237 pages. 1990.

Vol. 345: A. Cambini, E. Castagnoli, L. Martein, P Mazzoleni, S. Schaible (Eds.), Generalized Convexity and Fractional Programming with Economic Applications. Proceedings, 1988. VII, 361 pages. 1990.

Vol. 346: R. von Randow (Ed.), Integer Programming and Related Areas. A Classified Bibliography 1984–1987. XIII, 514 pages. 1990.

Vol. 347: D. Ríos Insua, Sensitivity Analysis in Multi-objective Decision Making. XI, 193 pages. 1990.

Vol. 348: H. Störmer, Binary Functions and their Applications. VIII, 151 pages. 1990.

Vol. 349: G.A. Pfann, Dynamic Modelling of Stochastic Demand for Manufacturing Employment. VI, 158 pages. 1990.

Vol. 350: W.-B. Zhang, Economic Dynamics. X, 232 pages. 1990.

Vol. 351: A. Lewandowski, V. Volkovich (Eds.), Multiobjective Problems of Mathematical Programming. Proceedings, 1988. VII, 315 pages. 1991.

Vol. 352: O. van Hilten, Optimal Firm Behaviour in the Context of Technological Progress and a Business Cycle. XII, 229 pages. 1991.

Vol. 353: G. Riccil (Ed.), Declslon Processes In Economics. Proceedings, 1989. III, 209 pages 1991.

Vol. 354: M. Ivaldi, A Structural Analysis of Expectation Formation. XII, 230 pages. 1991.

Vol. 355: M. Salomon. Deterministic Lotsizlng Models for Production Planning. VII, 158 pages. 1991.

Vol. 356: P. Korhonen, A. Lewandowski, J . Wallenius (Eds.), Multlple Crltena Decision Supporl. Proceedings, 1989. XII, 393 pages. 1991.

Vol. 358: P. Knottnerus, Linear Models with Correlaled Disturbances. VIII, 196 pages. 1991.

Vol. 359: E. de Jong, Exchange Rate Determination and Optimal Economlc Policy Under Various Exchange Rate Regimes. VII, 270 pages. 1991.

Vol. 360: P. Stalder, Regime Translations, Spillovers and Buffer Stocks. VI, 193 pages . 1991.

Vol. 361: C. F. Daganzo, Logistics Systems Analysis. X, 321 pages. 1991.

Vol. 362: F. Gehreis, Essays In Macroeconomics of an Open Economy. VII, 183 pages. 1991.

Vol. 363: C. Puppe, Distorted Probabilities and Choice under Risk. VIII, 100 pages . 1991

Vol. 364: B. Horvath, Are Policy Variables Exogenous? XII, 162 pages. 1991.

Vol. 365: G. A Heuer, U. Leopold-Wildburger. Balanced Silverman Games on General Discrete Sets. V, 140 pages. 1991.

Vol. 366: J. Gruber (Ed.), Econometric Decision Models. Proceedings, 1989. VIII, 636 pages. 1991.

Vol. 367: M. Grauer, D. B. Pressmar (Eds.), Parallel Computing and Mathematical Optimization. Proceedings. V, 208 pages. 1991.

Vol. 368: M. Fedrizzi, J. Kacprzyk, M. Roubens (Eds.), Interactive Fuzzy Optimization. VII, 216 pages. 1991.

Vol. 369: R. Koblo, The Visible Hand. VIII, 131 pages.1991.

Vol. 370: M. J. Beckmann, M. N. Gopalan, R. Subramanian (Eds.), Stochastic Processes and their Applications. Proceedings, 1990. XLI, 292 pages. 1991.

Vol. 371: A. Schmutzler, Flexibility and Adjustment to Information in Sequential Decision Problems. VIII, 198 pages. 1991.

Vol. 372: J. Esteban, The Social Viability of Money. X, 202 pages. 1991.